The OD Source Book:
A Practitioner's Guide

The OD Source Book:
A Practitioner's Guide

Robert M. Frame
Randy K. Hess
Warren R. Nielsen

Pfeiffer
& COMPANY

Amsterdam • Johannesburg • London
San Diego • Sydney • Toronto

To Joy, DeAnn, and Julie, without whose support
this book could not have been written

PREFACE

This work is based on the methods and style that we employ in our own practice in the field of organization development (OD). We see this perspective as useful in that it allows us to present descriptions of actual interventions, recommendations based on our experience, and observations regarding potential pitfalls. We also see it as helpful in that it may generate questions regarding OD practice theories that remain in force but are untested. Our presentation of problems related to intervention and collaboration is not aimed at redefining OD. Instead, we want to share insights from our experience with some of the more standard techniques and perhaps provide a novel treatment of OD methodology.

Given this approach, we claim no more for this book than what it represents: a collection of observations and ideas derived from our practice. Of necessity it depends on our own biases, and as a result we do not attempt to develop principles or theory. We do, however, hope that this detailed explanation of OD as we practice it will guide and inspire others as they develop their own approaches.

Robert M. Frame
Randy K. Hess
Warren R. Nielsen

Omaha, Nebraska
December, 1981

CONTENTS

INTRODUCTION

This book is about the use of organization development (OD) in improving organizations. Because it is intended for both beginning and experienced professionals who want to enhance their understanding and use of OD techniques, the primary emphasis is on practice. The book also includes efforts to explain the rationale underlying certain approaches and, thus, unavoidably contains some philosophy regarding the justification of our approach to OD. The major purpose, however, is not to develop a theory of OD, to expound the role of OD as a mechanism of change, or to review and evaluate the many approaches to OD that have been documented in the literature; rather, it is to provide the practitioner with information on a topic that the authors feel has been neglected—the step-by-step implementation of OD.

OD PHILOSOPHY VERSUS OD PRACTICE: A PERSPECTIVE

The Issue of Collaboration

Although collaboration is seen by many practitioners as the foundation of OD, it presents an important problem. Many of the more noted writers in the field have stressed collaboration as the main characteristic of successful OD efforts and have tended to define it as "involvement," "power sharing," "participation," and so forth. To some, OD is not in effect unless participation is visible. In fact, another common assumption about this characteristic is that the more democratic and participative the system, the more effective the OD activity.

The notion that collaboration is a defining characteristic of OD probably cannot be disputed. However, the application of this concept can lead to difficulties arising from differences between the practitioner's and the client's interpretation.

A Workable Philosophy of Collaboration

Success in an OD intervention can be thought of as an increase in collaboration throughout a system. However, collaboration does not necessarily mean constant involvement. The authors define collaboration as "a good-faith effort based on trust and a mature understanding of roles and pressures." Thus, in some cases collaboration may mean willingness to tolerate the quick and authoritarian actions of those in power who need to move in order to get the job done.

Much of the practice of OD is representative of a bias toward defining collaboration as movement toward a power-sharing, participative state such as Likert's "System-4" concept (Sashkin, 1981). The authors, having dealt with some rather authoritarian and closed ("System-1") organizations, have noted their own bias toward interventions that stress "opening up" and building trust in such systems before making other changes; in fact, in certain instances such interventions have been viewed as prerequisites to effective change in other areas. However, the basic goal of applying OD as advocated in this guide is to help organizations to understand a contingency approach to change. Given this goal, the practitioner's premise is that a manager can choose from a range of decision-making styles; some situations call for the participation of subordinates or colleagues, whereas other situations are more appropriately handled by means of an authoritarian or "System-1" approach. It is not impossible for a practitioner to behave in a manner consistent with both this goal and a preference for collaboration: The building of trust within a system can be encouraged when diagnosis has indicated that lack of trust is a problem, and managers can be urged to be authentic in their managing styles and to be aware of the hidden costs of an excessively authoritarian approach. In essence, then, we as practitioners can attempt to demonstrate to managers that the human aspects of their work worlds are extremely complex, that worthwhile alternatives to their current management approaches may exist, and that the most sensible way to deal with change is to be aware of the situation.

Collaboration in Practice: Problems of Unintended Results

Unfortunately, despite the efforts of many practitioners to emphasize the contingent nature of OD in management practice, managers often translate that focus on collaboration into principles that are not, in fact, advocated. In attempting to understand the causes of this misinterpretation, we must examine our past interventions.

Evidently, part of the problem lies in the design of interventions in situations in which we sense that collaboration between supervisors and subordinates needs improvement. Initial interventions in most of these instances are process oriented and focused on taking risks, giving and receiving feedback, and so forth. Designs for such interventions tend to emphasize viewing group members as resources, evaluating resources, analyzing assumptions regarding those who have the most accurate information, and using a consensus approach to decision making. This emphasis creates a misperception about collaboration that can be stated as follows: *Collaboration means constant participation in decisions.*

Practitioners sometimes heighten this misperception by modeling a leadership role that stresses orientation toward process, maximum participation, and the value of comments from many group members. Thus, the original misperception is carried even further: *Collaboration means that subordinates usually have better information than supervisors and should, therefore, make decisions for their supervisors.*

Of course, we as practitioners do not typically attempt to "muzzle" managers or keep them from expressing opinions in group discussions. However, in our continual efforts to involve everyone in the intervention process, we often tend to highlight ideas contributed by group members other than the manager. It is easy to see how this tendency, viewed in the context of a nondirective style of consulting, comes to be seen as the true meaning of collaboration and, therefore, as "the way to do OD."

As a result, both supervisors and subordinates often conclude that to conduct OD efforts properly, supervisors must not only *involve* subordinates in all decisions, but also *defer* to them in most situations. In effect, then, we often confuse our clients by impressing them with the value of involving subordinates, which seemingly diminishes the leadership role of the manager and culminates in the two misperceptions just discussed.

Another source of the misunderstanding surrounding collaboration is the fact that OD process interventions often exaggerate the manager's responsibility for developing a more open and trusting relationship in group and intergroup situations. The efforts of the practitioner to persuade the manager to examine his or her style, to check out his or her impact on the group, and to take the initiative in legitimizing open and honest feedback about work-related situations can create the impression that the manager is solely responsible for developing collaboration. Another misperception, therefore, is formulated: *Collaboration means that the supervisor alone takes action to build trust and openness.*

Obviously, the supervisor is a crucial element in the building of trust in work-group relationships; his or her style, if not confronted, occasionally can become an obstacle that the group never overcomes. Therefore, the practitioner tends to intervene in a manner that will ensure to a reasonable degree that the supervisor will begin the process of clearing away obstacles to openness and trust building. Unfortunately, however, such an approach merely sets the stage for collaboration that requires active support from the entire group to make the process effective. Thus, the impact of the OD effort can be greatly reduced by the misinterpretation that responsibility for building openness and trust lies only with the manager. The manager may work very hard at being more open and honest, at soliciting feedback, and so forth; but the group members may not follow his or her lead if they see such action as totally the manager's responsibility. Subsequently, out of frustration, the manager may lessen personal efforts toward openness, thereby convincing the group members that he or she is not serious about increasing trust.

Thus, as a result of much OD practice, clients come to believe that authoritarian practices must be completely eliminated and that subordinate participation should be total and constant. They also develop very frustrating expectations regarding the way in which supervisors should act. Because the reality in most organizations is that it is impossible to involve all or even most subordinates in decision making and that it is equally impossible for managers to effect trust and openness without the help of their subordinates, many clients conclude that OD is either a sham or simply unworkable.

RATIONALE FOR THIS BOOK

The authors, after witnessing the negative outcomes just described in their own practice and determining that such outcomes represent common pitfalls for OD practitioners, realized the need for a detailed guide to OD techniques and their application, with an emphasis on pinpointing practice difficulties and ways to avoid or minimize these difficulties.

A Guide to OD Techniques

The primary element in this book is the description of methodology for conducting OD activities. For each type of intervention discussed, specific steps are provided as well as the strategy related to those steps and the rationale for that particular approach.

Furthermore, the authors feel that much of the so-called "mystique" of OD and its technology stems from the tendency of practitioners to avoid writing about what they actually do and to emphasize instead the philosophical issues involved. The descriptions of

OD methods presented in this book, therefore, have been developed specifically for the practitioner who needs to know not only what a particular technique is designed to accomplish, but also how that technique is carried out. In addition to presenting specific procedural steps, the guidelines provided suggest potential problems of which the practitioner needs to be aware.

It is important to remember that there is no magic formula for success in any approach to OD intervention. Simply following the steps provided in this guide will not solve organizational problems; the practitioner also must possess the interpersonal skills to handle interventions effectively. Thus, the designs presented here are intended as tools for the interpersonally competent practitioner who desires to channel existing skills toward specific outcomes.

The Application of Techniques to Organizations

Because the approach taken in this book is based on the authors' actual experiences with organizations, it encompasses the issues and constraints that are common in today's busy, demanding, and complicated work environments. The techniques and strategies described have been applied to real organizational situations involving long-term relationships and numerous interventions.

The authors have worked with the managements of large and small, public and private organizations to solve problems in the *total system*. To clarify, important differences exist between single-intervention situations such as those involving management training and long-term, multi-intervention approaches built on analysis of total-system issues. Some practitioners teach OD skills to isolated groups, whereas others apply such skills to total departments, plants, divisions, or other systems. Although the authors have engaged in both types of activity, they view their learnings from a number of extended, multifaceted consulting relationships as particularly useful because such relationships are more reflective of the actual intent of OD. The focus of this guide, consequently, is systemic activity: recognizing tradeoffs, dealing with symptoms, matching interventions to goals, and establishing sequences of interventions.

Cautions Regarding Practice Difficulties

Finally, the authors feel that they have encountered certain types of complications often enough to risk declarations of characteristic problems associated with making the interventions advocated in this book. Suggestions of ways to avoid or minimize such problems are based on the authors' own experiences in evaluating their failure to identify and remove obstacles created by inaccurate assumptions. These suggestions include methods for testing perceptions of the meaning of OD and what it should or should not produce.

REFERENCE

Sashkin, M. An overview of ten management and organizational theorists. In J.E. Jones & J.W. Pfeiffer (Eds.), *The 1981 annual handbook for group facilitators*. San Diego, CA: University Associates, 1981.

PART I

FOUNDATIONS OF ORGANIZATION DEVELOPMENT

Part I, which consists of Chapters 2, 3, and 4, deals with the authors' view of the foundations of OD practice. Chapter 2 describes why OD efforts are launched, provides a detailed explanation of what OD is as opposed to what it is not, discusses the key elements of the process, and finally presents a model of OD that is contingent on organizational needs.

Chapter 3 concerns managerial motivation for becoming involved in OD. Motives that impair the OD process are described and categorized, as are motives that support and enhance the process. Ways to determine and respond to motivation are also discussed.

In Chapter 4 the authors deal with the subject of how to begin an OD effort. The steps involved in building a strategy are presented, along with related considerations. Advice is also given on ways to initiate an effort as well as ways to overcome patterns of failure.

A MODEL OF OD PRACTICE

Often it seems that almost any activity conducted for the purpose of developing individuals, units, or entire systems is called "organization development," indicating a great deal of confusion regarding the distinguishing characteristics of OD. The authors' experience suggests two criteria:

1. Organization development is invariably launched on the basis of a *felt need for action*, which, in turn, leads to *systematic planning* that allows for and builds on the following factors:

- The client's actual situation versus the desired situation;
- Interdependencies in the client system; and
- Specific changes required to progress toward the client's desired situation.

2. Both planning and implementation of interventions incorporate the value of *humanism*, which, in turn, leads to an emphasis on *collaboration.* Organization development has been described not only as a humanistic process (Bennis, 1969; Conner, 1977; Huse, 1975; Margulies & Raia, 1972), but also as a collaborative process between those effecting change and those affected by change (Argyris, 1970; Bennis, 1969). This approach represents an alternative to methods that tend to be unilaterally imposed, such as behavior modification (Luthans & Kreitner, 1975; Scott, 1977).

Figure 1 presents the key elements of the OD process, which consist of actions consistent with both criteria. It is the authors' contention that OD exists only when both sets of actions listed in Figure 1 take place. In contrast, when an intervention includes change processes that are based exclusively on felt needs and systematic planning, frequently it is predicated on the assumption that human perceptions of the contemplated change will be either favorable or largely irrelevant. Examples of such unilaterally imposed interventions undertaken by management without the collaboration of those affected include management by objectives (MBO) and measures aimed at job enrichment (Herzberg, 1966; Hackman, Oldham, Janson, & Purdy, 1975). Leading proponents of these potentially useful processes tend to believe that prior communication with the employees involved will raise

---

Portions of the model presented in this chapter are based on R.K. Hess and L.E. Pate, "A Contingency Model of Organization Development Change Processes," in *American Institute for Decision Sciences Proceedings* (Vol. 2), 1978, pp. 165-167. Used with permission.

Actions Consistent with
Humanistic Values
and Collaboration

- The perceptions, feelings, and attitudes of the people affected by a change are viewed as important and are taken into account when that change is planned.
- Those affected by a change are involved in the process of shaping that change.
- Important data about a change are shared with those affected by it.
- Those affected by a change have influence over the nature of that change (*when* and *how* it occurs and, to some extent, *what* occurs).
- Feedback is elicited from those who might be affected by a change.
- Feedback on the success of a change, the need for corrective action, and the need for maintenance activities is provided to those affected by that change.

Actions Consistent with
Systematic Planning
Based on Felt Needs

- Study and analysis are used to determine actual problems, feasible solution alternatives, and a ranking of alternatives.
- Objectives are considered in terms of their impact on the total organization.
- Interdependencies are noted and considered.
- Long-range as well as short-range impact is taken into account.
- The effects of a change on tasks, structure, technology, and processes involving people are considered.
- Concern is given to the implementation, review, and reinforcement of a change activity.

Figure 1. Key Elements of the OD Process

---

unrealistic expectations that may be violated if the planned change cannot be implemented (a belief that is not consistent with the authors' general experience). Thus, this type of intervention ignores humanism and collaboration.

Similarly, when an intervention consists of processes that place a high value on human involvement as the sole requirement for effective change, little or no careful consideration is given to the impact on the organizational structure or technology. Supervisors converted to the concept of participative management are often highly supportive of such interventions. This approach to organizational change represents an all-too-common misinterpretation of OD as strictly a "people-centered" movement implemented with a lack of regard for operating effectiveness or bottom-line performance. This misinterpretation may explain the virtual demise of T-groups and other laboratory-education methods in corporations during the past two decades (Campbell & Dunnette, 1968; Golembiewski & Blumberg, 1977).

In summary, processes that ignore one criterion or the other are both appropriate and effective in many situations, but they are *alternatives* to OD as defined here and as clarified in the following explanation of the authors' model.

A MODEL OF OD CONTINGENT ON ORGANIZATIONAL NEEDS

The authors' model of OD practice contrasts with those that frequently have been labeled the ".medical" or "clinical" models (Margulies & Raia, 1978). The clinical interpretation has led many in the field to describe OD as "medicine" for "unhealthy" organizations, thus placing the OD practitioner in the role of an organizational "physician" who applies processes that are offered as "cures." It is the authors' experience that the medical approach is both distracting and unhelpful because it tends to generate a defensive reaction on the part of clients, who object to being seen as "patients."

It seems more helpful to view OD as a multivariate process involving a number of interdependent steps or phases, each of which builds from the previous one. Each step of this process yields new data, which are subsequently evaluated and incorporated into data generated previously. Then objectives are reassessed, and decisions are made regarding the next step. Thus, OD cannot be accomplished with a single activity. Instead, it is an evolutionary process (Pate, 1979) that is contingent on successively emerging organizational needs; it adds options to those currently available within the organization, be they technical, structural, behavioral, or systemic. Given this definition, the organization is seen as *continually developing* rather than as "unhealthy," and the more positive view raises fewer defenses or unrealistic expectations.

Felt Needs and Shared Analysis

The client's felt need for action manifests itself in a variety of ways ranging from frustration with poor operating results to perceptions of "people problems." Whatever form it takes, without it no energy or resources are committed to OD, as experienced practitioners can attest. The initial role of the practitioner becomes one of working with organizational leaders to assist them with appropriate analysis of the felt need. To establish collaboration and to ensure the support of eventual change processes, those potentially affected by change are included in this procedure.

The practitioner can use any of a number of different methods to help to determine the exact nature of the felt need. For example, he or she can administer questionnaires, conduct surveys, employ observational techniques, ask employees to generate on-the-spot data, or analyze various performance indicators (absenteeism, turnover, production levels, and so forth) that are found in organizational records. Through these means data can be obtained on a variety of elements governing organizational life (Kimberly & Nielsen, 1975):

- Behavior (individual, subsystem, and system);
- Patterns and frequency of contact between individuals and groups;
- Role behavior and interdependence (the ways in which individuals and groups define their roles);
- The structure and process of decision making and problem solving;
- The organizational structure;
- The ways in which planned changes are (or are not) executed; and
- Attitudes and perceptions.

The resulting data indicate which organizational component(s) gave rise to the felt need. An organization consists of six major components:

1. *Groups*, which can be analyzed according to norms, relationships (both within and between), performance levels, work distribution, functions, priorities, and decision-making and problem-solving processes;

2. *Environment*, which is established by market, competitors, related organizations, government regulations, societal values, manpower potential, and social responsiveness;

3. *Technology*, which consists of knowledge, equipment, processes used, and the overall flow of activity;

4. *Structure*, which includes the reward system, hierarchy, patterns of contact between employees, the goals and purpose of the organization, policy and procedures, the financial system, the physical setting, decision-making mechanisms, size, and reporting relations;

5. *Individuals*, who possess unique biographics, skills, educational backgrounds, needs and motivational patterns, value systems, behavior patterns, and performance levels; and

6. *Tasks*, which reflect job-design elements, authority and responsibility, required skills, time requirements, motivational patterns, and work flow.

All six of these organizational components interact with and affect each other, as shown in Figure 2. Although any shared analysis leading to change efforts would not necessarily involve more than one or two of these components at a time, effective OD work calls for awareness of their interactions. For example, to interpret data to mean that individuals' skills need upgrading and then to proceed immediately to develop plans for skills training without considering the ways in which tasks and structure might affect the training results is to risk committing considerable resources to a project that is unlikely to meet real needs or to resolve underlying problems.

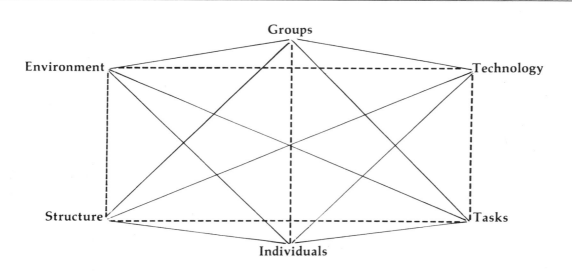

Figure 2. Interaction of Organizational Elements

Primary Change Targets

After shared analysis has revealed which organizational component(s) gave rise to the client's felt need and the desired change has been determined, it is necessary to establish which of the three organizational subsystems are necessary targets of the change process. These subsystems—the sociosystem, the process system, and the technosystem—represent three stages in the flow of events of the OD process. Each should be examined to determine whether it is already supportive of the desired change; if it is not, interventions should be conducted in that subsystem. These potential targets are defined as follows:

1. The *sociosystem* consists of the attitudes, values, and perceptions of the employees coupled with the climate in the organization, which is a function of openness, trust, cooperation, and self-direction.

2. The *process system* consists of the organization's decision-making, communication, and problem-solving vehicles, which incorporate such elements as problem definition, selection of solutions, utilization of resources, delegation, conflict management, goal setting, information sharing, and self-evaluation.

3. The *technosystem* consists of the organization's technical and structural aspects: formalized procedures, policies, and rules as well as the design of the organization, the structure of its jobs, the staffing patterns, physical facilities, equipment, tools, and operating technology (Leavitt, 1965).

All of these subsystems are of equal importance to the organization and to its employees. This fact is stressed because the authors' experience as well as that of other professionals reinforces the need to practice OD as a process incorporating and blending rational procedures (systematic planning) with democratic processes (humanistic values) to benefit both bottom-line production and people (Weisbord, 1981). In this way a balance is achieved between "humanistic normative approaches and a technocratic orientation" (Tichy & Sole, 1977) so that the organization's viability is ensured.

Plans for Change

In the authors' model, illustrated in Figure 3, the key OD values of systematic planning and humanism are operationalized. Each target subsystem is examined to determine whether interventions are required to bring it to a minimally acceptable state of demonstrated effectiveness. The initial step in the flow of the model is to collaborate with the client to obtain valid data (honest, accurate, reasonably complete information) about the *sociosystem*. Without such data no positive change will occur in any of the three subsystems. If the data affirm the existence of an effective sociosystem, no intervention into that subsystem is necessary; however, if the data establish the need for sociosystem improvement, staff-development interventions are necessary. Throughout the process of achieving staff development, which is detailed in Figure 3, the practitioner must ensure that OD values are operative.

Once evidence exists that the sociosystem is both producing valid data and improving in effectiveness, the next step is examination of the *process system* as a vehicle for augmenting and enhancing work in staff development. If interventions are deemed appropriate, they are planned and implemented. When the process system has been determined to be effective, the final target, the *technosystem*, is examined and addressed as necessary.

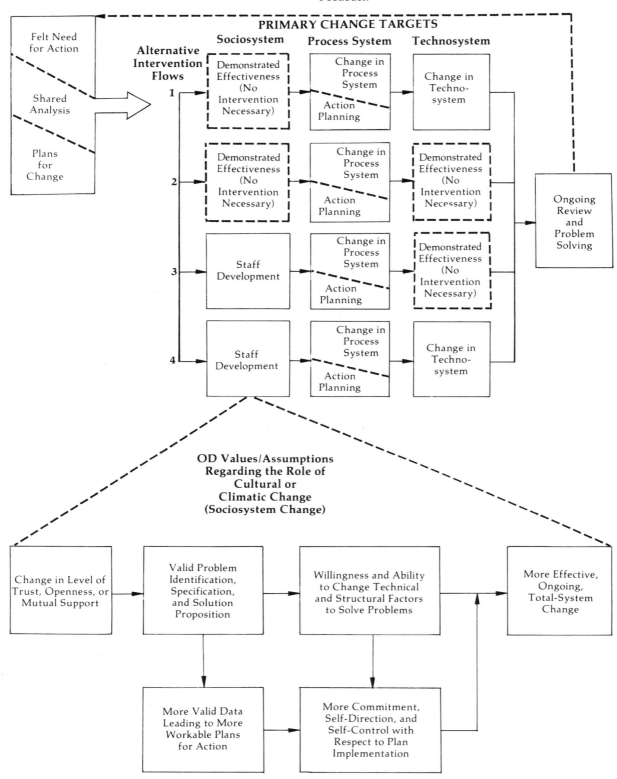

Figure 3. A Model of OD Contingent on Organizational Needs

Alternative Intervention-Flow Combinations

Figure 2 is intended to illustrate OD as encompassing alternative patterns or flows of change effort. Each flow pattern begins with the sociosystem as an appropriate initial phase in the execution of OD interventions, even if the felt need is oriented toward the process system or the technosystem. For example, shared analysis and plans for change may indicate no need for staff development; in this case the change effort proceeds on a collaborative basis to the process system and the technosystem, as indicated in alternative intervention flow 1 in Figure 3. In alternative intervention flow 2, the sociosystem of the organization is established as minimally effective, with people providing valid data about appropriate strategies to accomplish changes; it differs from alternative 1 in that technosystem intervention is not indicated. In alternatives 3 and 4 the need for appropriate OD interventions is determined for the sociosystem in the form of staff-development activity. Both entail a subsequent stage with planned interventions aimed at the process system, but only alternative 4 projects plans for changes in the technosystem.[1]

Figure 3 also depicts an ongoing review and problem-solving phase coupled with a feedback loop returning to the originating felt-need stage. This circular course reflects the fact that OD is a continual process, cyclical in nature, with one intervention frequently leading to the need for further work. The circular nature of the model as illustrated also reflects the fact that "quick fixes" and permanent solutions are not possible in today's dynamic organizations operating in changing environments. A key to the OD process and the effective application of the interventions detailed in Part II of this guide is the use of strategies and tactics to ensure periodic analysis, renewal, and ongoing maintenance.

REFERENCES

Argyris, C. *Intervention theory and method.* Reading, MA: Addison-Wesley, 1970.

Bennis, W. *Organization development: Its nature, origins and prospects.* Reading, MA: Addison-Wesley, 1969.

Campbell, J., & Dunnette, M. Effectiveness of T-group experiences in managerial training and development. *Psychological Bulletin,* 1968, *70,* 73-104.

Conner, P. A critical inquiry into some assumptions and values characterizing OD. *Academy of Management Review,* 1977, *2,* 635-644.

Golembiewski, R., & Blumberg, A. (Eds.). *Sensitivity training and the laboratory approach* (3rd ed.). Itasca, IL: F.E. Peacock, 1977.

Hackman, R., Oldham, G., Janson, R., & Purdy, K. A new strategy for job enrichment. *California Management Review,* 1975, *17*(4), 57-71.

Herzberg, F. *Work and the nature of man.* New York: World, 1966.

Huse, E. *Organization development and change.* St. Paul, MN: West, 1975.

Kimberly, J.R., & Nielsen, W.R. *Designing assessment strategies for OD.* Paper presented at the ASTD National Conference, Las Vegas, May 1975.

Leavitt, H. Applied organizational change in industry. In J. March (Ed.), *Handbook of organizations.* Chicago: Rand McNally, 1965.

---

[1]Additional flows or combinations of alternative intervention strategies that exclude the process system from active change efforts may occur. However, when such situations arise, the authors believe that no effective OD work is likely to be accomplished in the technosystem; it is doubtful that the problem solving needed for specific technosystem change would occur on a collaborative basis without the data that would surface as part of the process-system phase. Thus, the model presented in this guide is restricted to the four alternatives just explained.

Luthans, F., & Kreitner, R. *Organizational behavior modification*. Glenview, IL: Scott, Foresman, 1975.

Margulies, N., & Raia, A. *Organizational development: Values process and technology*. New York: McGraw-Hill, 1972.

Margulies, N., & Raia, A.P. *Conceptual foundations of organizational development*. New York: McGraw-Hill, 1978.

Pate, L.E. Development of the OCIR model of the intervention process. *Academy of Management Review*, 1979, 4, 281-286.

Scott, W. Leadership: A functional analysis. In J. Hunt & L. Larson (Eds.), *Leadership*. Carbondale: Southern Illinois University Press, 1977.

Tichy, N., & Sole, K. *Agents of planned change: A second look* (Working Paper 164). Graduate School of Business, Columbia University, 1977.

Weisbord, M.R. Some reflections on OD's identity crisis. *Group & Organization Studies*, 1981, 6(2), 161-175.

MANAGERIAL MOTIVATION

A factor that is crucial to the success of an OD effort is the managerial motivation for becoming involved. The potential for the mental set of managers to influence the use of OD and thus its integrity is illustrated by an incident that occurred during a workshop conducted by the authors.

> In the course of a question-and-answer session near the end of the workshop, the issue of fear arose. Subsequent discussion focused on the reluctance of employees in large corporations such as the one sponsoring the workshop to speak up when problems arise. After a few participants acknowledged that they attributed this reluctance to fear of reprisal, one senior-level participant asked very earnestly, "Tell me, gentlemen, how do you think we can use OD to beat down fear in this company?"

Although such comments can be humorous, they ought not to be overlooked when considering the prospects for OD within a domain influenced by such managers. Frequently they are indicative of a lightly veiled contempt for those members of the organization who are seen as the source of nagging and seemingly unsolvable problems, and usually they are based on a belief that power and bluster offer the only real options for achieving goals. Managers who lack an adequate understanding of what OD can and cannot be expected to accomplish become involved for the wrong reasons; often they see OD as a way to "straighten out" subordinates who are "misguided." This outlook obviously can cause considerable trouble during an OD effort: The client managers soon discover that the OD process cannot meet their expectations, and the effort either becomes sidetracked or fails completely, leaving the managers with serious doubts as to whether OD has any practical value.

The existence of these attitudes is understandable when examined in the context of organizational history. Often the traditional climate of an organization is perpetuated by a cycle of authoritarian leadership, promotion from within, and rewards for not questioning directives; consequently, levels of trust are low and risks are seldom taken. In this type of environment, in which employees seem to respond only to overt or implied threats, one can see how members of the organization develop negative behavior patterns and come to believe that such patterns are justified and necessary. Managers whose backgrounds lie in such traditions are often reluctant to explore their own reliance on authority or to challenge their approaches to motivating employees. Sometimes they simply regard OD as a convenient way to increase control through manipulation of subordinates—an interpretation that enables them to continue to harbor their low opinions of openness, trust, and authenticity.

In contrast, positive managerial motivation for launching OD is characterized by the absence of unrealistic expectations and a willingness to engage in self-examination. Managers who display this attitude are able to grasp the nature and extent of the impact of traditional norms on organizations. For example, during a recent OD workshop two high-level managers expressed frustration about their colleagues' desire to solve employee-motivation difficulties with some type of "quick fix" and without becoming involved in or committed to any long-term effort to deal with the underlying problems.

> After listening to several ambitious, "quick-fix" suggestions, one of the managers confronted her peers with this concern by remarking, "Let's face it—it's taken us fifty years to mess up this company, and we're not going to straighten it out in fifty days!"
>
> One of her colleagues reflected on similar attitudes manifested by his on-line management subordinates after launching an OD effort. During a meeting to review progress, he told these subordinates, "You seem to want OD *up* but not OD *down*. OD *up* is great because you enjoy being able to talk freely and openly with me. However, the evidence as I read it is that you don't really want your subordinates actively involved because you don't want feedback from them."

Managerial motivation can vary widely between this extreme and the one described previously. Basically, however, a motivation can be considered to belong to one of two categories:

1. Those that are questionable in that they tend to impair the success of an OD effort; and

2. Those that are supportive and tend to enhance success.

MOTIVES THAT IMPAIR THE OD PROCESS

In each of the following motive classifications, the manager described has elected to begin an OD effort based on an understanding of the process that is either indicative of inadequate information or deliberately misconstrued to serve as an expediency. In either case the understanding is insufficient for the proper utilization of OD to achieve either developmental or remedial purposes.

Motive 1: To Obtain "OD Training" for Subordinates

The manager who seeks to obtain "OD training" for subordinates characteristically believes that OD is a new program designed to produce attitudinal change in a desired direction. He or she may also feel that it can do little or no harm to try the "program," which is assumed to be highly structured and prepared in advance. The OD process is viewed as one in which employees passively listen to presentations that are supposed to motivate them. Thus, the general image of the practitioner is that of an inspiring lecturer who provides insight, advice, and so forth.

This type of manager has little awareness of real organizational problems and even less confidence that OD can effect real change in the organizational situation. When OD is approached with this attitude, it is ultimately perceived as a diversion to be tolerated and then ignored when completed.

Motive 2: To Offer OD as an Extra Reward

This motive is characteristic of a manager who has some budget money to spend, wants to use it to show appreciation to subordinates, and believes that an off-site OD event constitutes a reward in the form of a reprieve from the regular work routine. Thus, OD is seen as a recreational and/or socializing event run by a practitioner with good social skills. The connection of OD to the real problems at the work place is perceived as very weak; it is assumed that OD relates only to morale issues. As a result the effort is not taken seriously in terms of operational priorities.

Motive 3: To Be Included in the Trend Toward OD

This motive is indicative of political acuity as well as a desire to conform. Managers who are thus motivated believe that it is fashionable and "the in thing" to demonstrate concern for subordinates, and often they undertake an OD effort in response to pressure from various sources to adopt contemporary practices. Organization development is viewed in terms of a fashionable or gala event at which the practitioner is expected to serve as an articulate and witty master of ceremonies. In this type of situation, the practitioner may, in fact, be complimented for being so "advanced."

Such motivation reflects little understanding of OD and may result in unfulfilled expectations. Awareness of real organizational problems may exist, but OD is not perceived as a way to address these problems; consequently, little resource commitment is likely to result.

Motive 4: To Gain Approval and Advancement

An extension of the previous motive, this one centers in the manager's desire to curry favor with superiors, to make the right impression, to appear progressive and concerned, and to ensure that his or her image is consistent with what is expected. Such a manager tends to view OD as a gimmick that is part of a career-advancement strategy; this gimmick is employed to help subordinates to learn how to behave so that the manager can gain recognition and approval. The practitioner who participates in this fantasy becomes a potential co-conspirator in furthering the manager's career.

In this case the manager is usually aware of the real problems in the organization but does not link OD to their solution. The probable results of an OD effort conducted under these circumstances include little or no real commitment, raised employee expectations, and eventual cynicism.

Motive 5: To Boost Employee Morale

The manager who manifests this motive feels that some activity is needed to raise the spirits of the employees, to convince them of their importance, and to show them that the organization really cares about them. The assumption is that an OD effort will persuade employees that their management is not so insensitive as they perceive. In effect, OD is thought of as a form of rally that will generate political support, stress the positive aspects of the organization, and establish a forum for pep talks. The practitioner is thus seen as a cheerleader who stimulates enthusiasm. Low morale is the primary problem of concern to such a manager, who perceives OD as a superficial solution that will "buy time" until his or her next job change.

Motive 6: To Learn How to Be Nicer

This motive is characteristic of managers who have been conditioned by years of autocratic leadership and suddenly become aware that top management no longer supports this style— at least in theory. The message they receive is that they need to show more appreciation for and interest in their subordinates, to exude more positive emotion, and to improve human relations. Although such managers often view this trend as coddling employees, like good soldiers they resign themselves to cooperating as instructed. The OD process is thus perceived as a form of innocuous charm school, with the practitioner serving as a human-relations theorist who facilitates activities for the purpose of improving work etiquette. The manager who holds these opinions is probably aware of morale problems but is unlikely to feel that OD can significantly influence the deeper, underlying concerns. An OD effort based on such attitudes will probably produce raised expectations and eventual skepticism when nothing concrete or permanent occurs in the way of behavioral change.

Motive 7: To Assuage Curiosity About OD and to Try Something New

The manager who is acting on the basis of curiosity feels that OD cannot really hurt anything and might be fun; he or she is usually in favor of any type of developmental activity. Organization development appears to be a fascinating, enticing idea or managerial toy, and activities related to OD are seen as opportunities for new experiences in human development. The practitioner, therefore, is expected to play the role of Santa Claus by supplying games and tricks to enjoy.

This type of manager may or may not be aware of serious organizational issues but seldom links them to the OD process. During this type of effort, real problems may surface but are not dealt with, resulting in cynicism born of unfulfilled expectations.

Motive 8: To Sell Unpopular Changes

The belief underlying this motive is that because employees are not mature enough to understand organizational needs, it is a waste of time to consult them about related changes; instead, management should make decisions independently and then try to win support for actions taken. A further assumption is that efforts to build employee loyalty will pay off in less questioning of changes determined by management. The OD process is thus viewed as a form of advertising promotion or political campaign conducted by the practitioner, who acts as a promoter of carefully orchestrated strategies.

Unlike those described thus far, this type of manager is acutely aware of potential problems in the organization and feels that a strong connection exists between their solution and the OD process. Organization development thus becomes a sales program with predictable results: resentment, cynicism, and increased resistance to the very changes being sold.

Motive 9: To Promote Employee Conformance

The manager who seeks to promote subordinate compliance characteristically clings to Theory-X beliefs (McGregor, 1966). Certain employees are seen as unproductive and maladjusted, and OD is viewed as a useful control device for manipulating or even shocking them into acceptable behavior. The practitioner, therefore, becomes a therapist, a trouble-shooter, or a "hired gun." Managers thus motivated are often acutely aware of morale problems and believe that the solution lies in an OD effort to communicate the organizational facts of life and to rehabilitate malcontents by forcing them to change their attitudes. The probable results of such an effort are fear and its related consequences, including a closed atmosphere, distrust, and further resistance of a more covert nature.

Motive 10: To Avert Personal Disaster

This motive is characteristic of managers who are under great pressure either to change or to produce results that are not forthcoming. They see OD as a panacea, a last-chance miracle cure to save them from any number of punishments, including the loss of their jobs. Often they feel the need to improve costs, quality, or profits quickly and to be able to show measures of improvement immediately. Organization development is perceived as a means to achieve quick payoffs, and the practitioner is thought of as a savior who will exorcise threatening demons. The manager who holds this view has an extreme awareness of real problems in the system and believes that OD is the only viable approach to solving these problems.

An effort conducted under these circumstances will probably result in the development of unrealistic goals and timetables, which, in turn, will lead to failure. Ultimately, all activities will come to a halt, and disillusionment and panic will ensue.

MOTIVES THAT SUPPORT AND ENHANCE THE OD PROCESS

In contrast to the negative motives just discussed, several bases for managerial involvement represent a more legitimate type of felt need that provides the requisite support for the OD process. These motivation categories are indicative of more realistic and, thus, more productive views of OD and the practitioner's role. Chances for positive results in efforts based on these motives are much higher than those associated with negative motives.

Motive 1: To Investigate Problems

The manager who enters an OD effort on the basis of this motive recognizes the fact that the organization is experiencing continuing problems. However, he or she also is aware that current statements of these problems are couched in terms that make solution improbable and wonders whether the real problems are, in fact, not being voiced. This type of manager relies heavily on intuition and wants to explore the situation to see whether OD can help to define the real problems. Organization development is thus viewed as an exploratory, analytical device; OD activities are perceived as cautious, judicious efforts to increase available problem data by opening communication and generating upward feedback within the organization. When an effort is conducted on this basis, the practitioner becomes a co-investigator. At the outset the manager senses that OD may have a strong potential for helping, but he or she is not yet certain.

Motive 2: To Test OD as a Helpful Approach

The manager whose motive is to test the usefulness of OD characteristically sees human problems as the underlying or causal base for numerous other problems being experienced but is uncertain whether OD will confirm this perception. Such a manager generally feels that he or she has never been able to break through to the real problem areas, that subordinates are holding back and hesitant to say what they really think, and that all employees should be more involved in problem-solving and decision-making processes. Thus, an OD effort is initiated as a test project to determine whether real problem solving will occur; each activity is fully supported and carefully monitored. The practitioner is viewed as a potential source of creativity, a catalyst, and a resource. The manager is acutely aware of problems and perceives a definite linkage between these problems and OD, although he or she remains uncertain about the extent of this linkage until the testing has been accomplished.

Motive 3: To Undergo an Educational Process

This motive, like the two preceding ones, is based on a felt need for learning. It is also indicative of a genuine respect for education and a strong belief in the connection between learning and the solution of significant problems. In this case the manager wants to achieve a full understanding of basic OD values, the rationale behind activities, the commitments that must be made, and the consequences before launching an effort. He or she feels that OD may be helpful but wants to be certain about the practitioner's assessment of limitations. Thus, the OD process is seen as a mysterious but potentially valuable management strategy; activities are thought of as including learning and planning events as well as careful evaluations of various process options. The practitioner is considered to be both teacher and co-assessor.

Typically this type of manager is reasonably aware of real organizational problems, but final judgment regarding the effects of OD on such problems is reserved until results have been obtained. As is the case with motives 1 and 2, the chances for positive results are great, although problems may arise due to the manager's orientation toward *learning*; motives 4 through 6, in contrast, involve an orientation toward *doing*.

Motive 4: To Shape Change

This motivation reflects a clear realization that changes are necessary and that they will affect many people. Such a manager reveals a genuine desire to receive employee input about contemplated changes and to reduce the fear associated with these changes. He or she wants to involve employees at all levels in the process of defining, implementing, and promoting commitment to change.

Organization development is viewed as a highly respected strategy for effecting change, and individual activities are seen as proactive steps that are taken to alleviate anxiety regarding impending changes. The practitioner is thought of as a sensitive change agent whose responsibility is to help the manager to unfreeze communications. The manager is acutely aware of potential resistance to change and perceives a strong linkage between this resistance and the OD process.

Motive 5: To Foster Preventive Maintenance

A manager who manifests this motive believes that the organization is doing well, that interpersonal relationships are generally good, and that these positive conditions should be preserved through some mechanism that ensures ongoing future commitment. He or she is aware of the constant need to develop plans for the future and to involve employees at as many levels as possible in maintaining a state of alertness for early-warning signals of deterioration in processes such as communication, delegation, and so forth. Such a manager also recognizes the consequences of maintaining a fast pace in the organization without periodic checks on employee feelings about such matters as involvement and commitment. Organization development is seen as offering various ways to accomplish such maintenance checks. The practitioner becomes a reasonably objective resource, a co-analyst, and a helpful critic. The manager is aware of the high potential for problems related to heavy work loads and perceives a strong linkage between these problems and OD.

Motive 6: To Build Organizational Strength

This motive is characteristic of the manager who realizes that the organization is functioning well, but that vehicles must be established for continual re-examination in order to sustain excellence in performance. An additional goal is to identify and to tap human resources that have not been used at an optimum level. This type of manager also supports the inclusion of as many employees as possible in decision making and planning.

These beliefs are so strongly held that the manager is willing to risk not only employee assessment of current strengths and weaknesses but also employee evaluation of alternative approaches. Thus, the manager views OD as a fine-tuning process and the practitioner as a co-analyst and catalyst. He or she is also acutely aware of the potential for slippage from the level of effectiveness currently enjoyed and feels that OD can probably enhance the strengths that are already present in the organization.

Motive 7: To Help to Remedy Human-Resource Problems

This motive and the two that follow tend to be oriented toward *reinforcing* both the *learning* and *doing* aspects of OD. Managers who display this motive recognize organizational difficulties in the human-resource arena that may be worsening but are not unsolvable. Usually such a manager admits that people are not addressing these difficulties but supports their doing so via OD, which is seen as the best option for resolution. Organization-development activities are viewed as necessary albeit sometimes painful or challenging steps required to analyze issues fully. The practitioner's role is seen as being that of an expert in interpersonal relations, a confronter, and a human-systems analyst. This type of manager is not only acutely aware of employee problems; he or she also perceives a strong link between OD and resolution of these problems.

Motive 8: To Change the Organizational Climate

Managers of this type are anxious to ensure that the climate of the organization fosters the meeting of organizational objectives. They express a genuine desire to build trust between individuals and groups in order to reduce "backbiting" and destructive conflict. In addition, they want to increase commitment to objectives, build greater ownership of personal behavior, and reduce defensive posturing. In essence, such a manager seeks to enhance collaborative and problem-solving capabilities throughout the organization.

Organization development is thought to be both a philosophy and a strategy for examining current behavior patterns and influencing norms; activities are viewed as interrelated steps aimed at long-range improvement in climate. The practitioner is seen as a strategist, an analyst, and an interpersonal-behavior expert. For this type of manager, problem awareness centers in concern for the general organizational climate rather than in the specific problems created by that climate; OD is perceived as having great potential for climatic improvement.

Motive 9: To Revitalize the Organization

The chief concerns of this type of manager are lackluster performance and mediocrity in the organization. He or she wants to rekindle employee interest and involvement in the organization's structure, tasks, objectives, and philosophy. Needs are expressed for new patterns of behavior: more introspection, confrontation of narrow perspectives and broadening of vision, questioning of organizational processes as opposed to blind obedience to rules, and increased efforts to meet organizational objectives as a result of a sense of ownership.

Organization development is believed to represent a strategy for improving the organization's use of resources, particularly through emphasis on employee self-assessment; activities are seen as steps that are taken to build awareness of problem performance patterns and to elicit support for changes related to these patterns. The practitioner serves as a catalyst and a guide in the process of change assessment. Managerial awareness of problems is acute at a broad level, and OD is strongly related as a potential solution mechanism.

HOW TO DETERMINE MOTIVATION

Although no one has the ability to determine absolutely the motives of another person, a process does exist whereby sufficient information can be elicited to provide a workable assessment of motivation. To a certain extent, motivation can be screened during the preliminary contracting session. The authors have found it advisable to request that this session be attended by the potential client manager, his or her immediate supervisor, and at least some of his or her subordinates; if the manager seems reluctant to schedule a meeting with both the supervisor and subordinates present, the practitioner can interpret this reluctance as a significant sign of inappropriate motivation. Sufficient time should be allotted for this meeting to allow for a discussion of reasonable depth about felt needs, important issues, reactions, and concerns regarding the ideas expressed.

To inquire into motives, the practitioner can ask questions such as the following:

- Why are you interested in exploring OD as an activity for your organization?
- If such an effort were launched, what end results would you expect or hope to achieve?
- What past developmental activities have you felt good about and why?
- What past activities have you viewed as poor investments and why?
- If you had complete organizational power, what would you change and why?
- What concerns do you have about the possibility of engaging in an OD effort?
- Why was I specifically chosen rather than someone else?
- What is your understanding of the motives of others in the organization for considering this effort? How do you feel about these motives?
- What specific role would you expect me to play in this effort?

While those in attendance at the session are answering these questions, the practitioner should exercise active-listening skills. In responding to these answers, it is best at this point to avoid expressions of skepticism and to concentrate instead on *reflecting*, which consists of restating in one's own words what has just been suggested. This technique helps the practitioner to maintain a supportive atmosphere during the question-and-answer segment of the meeting.

By uncovering the motives for considering the use of OD processes, the practitioner can determine whether those present have a reasonably clear and realistic understanding of OD and what might be expected. After this determination has been made, it is important to react honestly and forthrightly to any personal concerns that may have developed regarding motivation, allowing time for the client representatives to clarify their positions or to correct misunderstandings. If it becomes obvious after further discussion that the motives involved are likely to cause problems later, such motives must be confronted.

RESPONDING TO MANAGERIAL MOTIVATION

Obviously, confrontation is not always easy. The practitioner's desire to be helpful, to obtain a contract, and to avoid offending potential clients who actually do need help tends to build pressure in this type of situation. Another frequently encountered circumstance that can make confrontation even more difficult is the fact that the organizational representatives are under pressure to launch an OD effort. However, the practitioner who avoids confrontation and then helps to implement a less-than-successful project may experience serious regrets about failing to voice uneasiness at the outset.

The practitioner who has established a clear conceptual framework concerning the appropriate use of OD will find it less difficult to confront questionable motivation in a supportive manner. The preceding discussions of specific motives can serve as guidelines in the development of personal ideas about conditions that are likely to lead to success or failure. It is important not only to express concerns about motives but also to make one's own position as clear as possible. The following information should be shared with potential clients:

- Personal views and concerns about appropriate and inappropriate motivation;
- Reactions to client expectations regarding what can and cannot be accomplished through OD activity;

- Potential negative consequences of OD efforts that are either poorly motivated or poorly conceived and executed; and
- Personal expectations and requirements for launching an OD effort.

Although using this candid approach with potential clients may create short-term pressure for the practitioner, in the long run it can pay real dividends by laying the basis for the comfortable and mutually supportive relationship necessary to achieve success in an OD effort.

The form that confrontation takes usually depends on the following factors:

- The level of openness achieved during the discussion;
- The perceived receptivity to feedback on the part of those present;
- The apparent level of credibility enjoyed at this point by the practitioner; and
- The practitioner's opinion as to whether the impairing motive is susceptible to influence and change.

Without question some intuition is involved in judging these matters. However, intuition and personal judgment are integral to the practice of OD, and the successful practitioner learns to rely heavily on his or her internal feelings and evaluations of circumstances.

Immediate Confrontation of Impairing Motives

The practitioner can confront an impairing motive by offering direct and immediate feedback if it seems likely that the recipient will react with acceptance, interest, and willingness to do what is necessary for the success of the project. In the authors' experience, about one third of the situations involving impairing motives will lend themselves to this response. Such feedback need not be given in an accusatory manner; instead, the practitioner can use "I messages" (Gordon, 1978) and/or active-listening techniques, which reduce the possibility of a defensive reaction and open the way for a cooperative project design incorporating interventions that protect against the negative results associated with the motive. (See Chapters 5, 6, and 7 for specific intervention alternatives.)

To deliver this feedback effectively, the practitioner must explain clearly why the motive is inappropriate, how it might damage an OD effort, and how to safeguard against potentially damaging effects through specific interventions or through further joint analysis. In suggesting specific interventions, it is important to point out the probable results of these interventions and to clarify the rationale behind a project design sequence. This explanation provides the organizational representatives with an opportunity either to accept or to reject the project design on the basis of a good understanding in advance of the consequences of the decision. Thus, the problems normally generated by the motive should be minimized.

Delayed Confrontation of Impairing Motives

When dealing with the impairing motives of clients who do not seem receptive to feedback, delayed confrontation is more appropriate. This approach allows time for the organizational representatives to reflect on the discussion and for the practitioner to develop a strategy for avoiding the consequences of the impairing motive. Although the practice of delaying confrontation involves some risk that the client may withdraw, the authors have seldom found this to be the case. Generally the practitioner is afforded the opportunity for further face-to-face discussion.

One way to employ this method is to indicate a desire to think about what has been said and to meet again at a later date to discuss an oral proposal for a project that will ensure that the determined needs are met. In this way the practitioner can formulate the confrontation into an organized presentation, thereby increasing the probability of client acceptance of any necessary interventions. As an alternative, the practitioner can state plans to summarize in writing his or her understanding of the project as discussed thus far, indicating that specific recommendations will be included for review by and discussion with the client. This alternative permits the practitioner to confront the motive as clearly as possible in terms of design recommendations.

To illustrate what is meant by "design recommendations," a situation in which the practitioner is faced with the impairing motive "to boost employee morale" may be considered. Success in the OD effort is predicated on the practitioner's completion of the following activities:

1. Ascertaining the basis for assumptions that employees need some sort of motivator;
2. Proposing a diagnostic-based intervention to confirm or to negate the assumption that the problem is, in fact, related to employee morale (see Part II for specific examples);
3. Further proposing that a response to employee needs be planned only after additional data have been obtained and jointly interpreted; and
4. Suggesting some alternative intervention responses if analysis produces certain results.

By taking this approach, the practitioner introduces the potential clients to a basic OD process approach consistent with the model presented in Chapter 2 and simultaneously confronts questionable motivation in a potentially productive manner. If the organizational representatives balk at what is being proposed at any point during this or the ensuing discussion, this hesitancy provides the practitioner with an opportunity to deal with the impairing motive on the basis of *data* rather than *values*. In other words, most managers are less likely to become defensive when dealing with action- or task-oriented proposals than they are when presented with more abstract ones that can be interpreted as challenging their personal values.

REFERENCES

Gordon, T. *Leadership effectiveness training.* New York: Wyden, 1978.

McGregor, D.M. A philosophy of management. In W.G. Bennis & E.H. Schein (Eds.), with the collaboration of C. McGregor, *Leadership and motivation: Essays of Douglas McGregor.* Cambridge, MA: M.I.T. Press, 1966.

4

HOW TO BEGIN AN OD EFFORT

A successful, long-term, organizational-change project invariably begins with and is guided by a conscientiously and deliberately planned strategy. The practitioner's most critical task consists of building this strategy and ensuring that all contemplated interventions and activities are consistent with it. The purpose of this chapter is to outline the concepts behind strategy building, to present some approaches to initiating OD efforts, and to suggest ways to avoid or at least minimize the probability of becoming involved in failure patterns.

A DEFINITION OF "STRATEGY"

An organizational-change strategy is a comprehensive plan based on a thorough analysis of organizational needs and goals. It is designed to bring about specific changes and to ensure that appropriate steps are taken to maintain those changes. Included in it are definitions of end objectives, outlines of specific actions designed to produce the desired outcomes, time frames, and an evaluation or monitoring system. The strategy must specify alternative as well as primary interventions and take into consideration the power and influence dynamics of the organization.

It may be useful to point out that specific interventions, such as team building and job redesign, are not strategies. Interventions, unlike strategies, are simply activities with limited end objectives. Practitioners who confuse interventions with strategies seldom exert significant, long-term impact on organizational performance. If real organizational change is to be achieved and organizational performance improved, interventions must be used only as parts of an overall strategy.

GENERAL STEPS IN BUILDING A STRATEGY

Because circumstances vary among organizations, organizational-change strategies can vary as well. Similarly, the steps in strategy building may differ from organization to organization. Nevertheless, it is possible to identify certain general steps in this process.

1. *Defining the Change Problem.* In this step information is gathered regarding the performance of the organization and deterrents to desired performance levels. Factors that might be identified as hindrances include job designs, reward structures, skill levels, organizational structure, value systems, and so forth. Care must be taken at this stage not

to confuse symptoms with causes. For example, absenteeism may reduce performance levels; but, before progress can be made, the reasons for absenteeism must be determined.

2. *Determining Appropriate Change Objectives.* In this step change objectives are clearly and specifically defined, in both behavioral and quantitative terms, so that they are appropriate to and consistent with the particular organization. Too often a practitioner initiates standard interventions without having identified what needs to be accomplished or changed. Spending time in determining objectives increases the probability for success and enhances the practitioner's image as a contributor to the organization.

3. *Determining the System's and Subsystems' Readiness and Capacity to Change.* Nothing is more discouraging or detrimental to a change effort than reaching the middle of a project and discovering that the organization or a specific group within it is not ready or able to change. Analyzing readiness, willingness, and capacity before project initiation can help the practitioner to determine where to start and which interventions to use. Many times a change effort fails not because the organization cannot be changed, but because the practitioner starts with the wrong part of the system or does not take into account the relationships among readiness, willingness, and capacity. The authors have found it useful to gauge each key manager in this respect as well as each major area or function.

4. *Determining Key Subsystems.* In this step the total organization is reviewed to determine its key parts and its key personnel. To be successful in an OD effort, the practitioner must focus on those groups within the organization that exert the greatest impact on organizational performance and on those managers who influence the direction of the organization.

5. *Assessing One's Own Resources.* Assessing personal skills, talents, and emotional and social needs is not only consistent with meeting real organizational needs; it also assists the practitioner in maintaining an ethical stance. No practitioner can do well in all situations or with all interventions. However, the practitioner who takes stock of personal strengths and weaknesses before selecting a strategy is better able to determine which projects "fit" his or her abilities and which do not; consequently, it is easier to determine which activities to conduct oneself and which to refer to other practitioners, thereby matching the right resources with particular organizational needs.

6. *Selecting an Approach and Developing an Action Plan for Reaching Objectives.* In selecting an approach to an effort and in planning the individual steps for implementation, the practitioner must be concerned with which interventions to use, where in the organization to start, who is to be involved in the effort, how much time is required, and how the effort will be monitored. In view of the fact that organizational change is a process and that the practitioner must remain flexible and responsive to new developments, it is helpful to establish a flow diagram that accounts for each step. This practice enables the practitioner to analyze the progress of the effort and whether it is leading where intended. In addition, it enables managers to become intimately involved in the process and convinces them that the practitioner is, indeed, committed to reaching specific objectives that will benefit the organization.

STRATEGY CONSIDERATIONS

While building a change strategy, the practitioner should keep in mind the following organizational dynamics or change requirements.

1. *Unmet Needs or Goals.* The selection of specific interventions should be based on client responses regarding problems that are not being solved or goals that are not being reached. Managers and organizations readily respond to proposals that address acknowledged needs.

2. *Support System.* Of major importance in the success of an OD project is the practitioner's initial identification of supportive forces in the organization and his or her subsequent commitment to working with those forces. A project is seldom successful when an attempt is made to influence the total organization at once.

3. *Chance for Success.* The entire OD effort as well as each related activity should represent some chance for success. As obvious as this concept is, it is amazing how often projects are launched on the basis of little or no hope for success. To change an organization, a series of victories must be won. The practitioner is seldom given a second chance if the first activity is not at least moderately successful.

4. *Multiple Entry.* Organizations of any size have a tremendous capacity to withstand change. Many times such an organization experiences a short disturbance of the status quo as a result of an OD effort and then settles back into its original patterns. This problem of inertia can be dealt with through the use of multiple entry points. Although care must be exercised and planning must be deliberate, change in a larger organization is more likely to be accomplished if pressure is exerted on several different facets of its operation.

5. *Critical Mass.* One of the purposes for using multiple entry points is to bring about a critical mass. Just as a chain reaction builds sufficient force to produce a major result, so is an organization changed through the development of a strong and building thrust. A strategy must be built in such a way as to plan for and cause the occurrence of a critical mass.

6. *Organizational Control.* The chances for success in an OD effort are greater when the practitioner works with individuals or groups that have some autonomy or control over their own operations.

7. *Appropriate Levels of Involvement.* Careful consideration must be given to developing and providing for the appropriate involvement of managers and other individuals who will be affected by the proposed changes. Attention must be centered on those who need to be active in decision making, those who need to be given information, and those who need to provide input for evaluation.

8. *Communication to All Levels.* It is useful to develop plans for communicating intentions, goals, and progress to the entire organization. In one major project in the auto industry, for example, a biweekly, one-page update was given to all employees. This update had a marked impact on reducing resistance to the project and opening doors for suggestions and input.

9. *Determination of Feasibility.* Mechanisms must be established not only for letting key people know about change plans, but also for enlisting the aid of these people in determining the feasibility of plans. One of the biggest traps in building change strategies is planning in a vacuum.

10. *Linking with Internal Change Agents.* Most client organizations include employees who are responsible for organizational change and improvement. A practitioner's strategy is much more likely to succeed if he or she devises ways to coordinate efforts with those of personnel such as engineers, quality-control experts, designers, financial analysts, and so forth. Major organizational change is greatly enhanced by linking change teams from several disciplines or functions.

INITIATING THE EFFORT

After building a strategy, the practitioner is ready to select an approach for initiating the effort. Several alternatives exist, and combinations of these approaches can even be appropriate in many situations. Each approach presents certain advantages and disadvantages. It should be emphasized, however, that the success potential of any of the following approaches is greatly enhanced if the approach is used as a part of an overall strategy.

Selection of a Winner

With this approach the practitioner selects a project that is associated with a high probability of success and little chance of failure. Such a project might be an intergroup activity, for example, conducted under the following conditions:

- The two groups that participate need to interact more effectively;
- Both groups perceive this need; and
- Both groups are reasonably skilled at and committed to problem solving.

The advantages of this approach include low risk for the practitioner as well as the organization; a potentially high, quick return; and the opening of doors to other opportunities as a result of early success. However, among the disadvantages is the fact that the practitioner may be perceived as simply being in the right place at the right time rather than as working diligently on the organization's behalf. In addition, the problems addressed by the project may be seen as minor or of relatively little impact. Finally, those involved in the project may be perceived as special or as "different" from the rest of the employees.

Use of a Power Play

This approach involves starting with the most influential and powerful group in the organization. A suitable project might be a team-building activity conducted with the manager of this group and his or her staff.

The associated advantages are a high potential for change because of the target group's power to implement the change as well as a high return or impact attributable to the group's control over numerous variables. Still another advantage is the fact that if the project is successful, the practitioner gains a great deal of credibility, as does the OD process.

One of the disadvantages afforded by this approach is that it may make an overly powerful group even more so, thereby threatening the rest of the organization. Another negative result is that the practitioner may be seen as part of the organizational power structure. In addition, if such a project fails, there is high risk to the organization and to the future of other OD projects.

Limitation Through a Pilot Project

In using this approach the practitioner proposes and gains acceptance for completing a particular project that is limited to one or two areas of the organization. Examples include a job-development project accomplished in one department or a team-skills workshop conducted for a particular level within the organization.

Several advantages are associated with the pilot-project approach. It is often more acceptable to key managers than a large-scale effort, and its limitation in scope affords greater manageability. It also gives the practitioner an opportunity to demonstrate what can be done; and, if the initial effort is successful, the practitioner will find it easier to intervene in other parts of the organization on the strength of this success.

In contrast, such a project may be seen as successful only because it is "special." It also may be rejected on the basis that it is threatening to the rest of the organization. Under these conditions further intervention may become difficult due to skepticism about activities that were "not invented here."

Concentration on a Business Problem

With this approach an attempt is made to concentrate on attacking an acknowledged business problem such as turnover, absenteeism, poor quality, high scrap, or deteriorating relationships. An example of such a project might be the use of problem-solving quality circles to improve product quality.

One advantage of this approach is that the effort is perceived as legitimate because it is directed toward an acknowledged problem. As with the pilot-project approach, the chance for success is enhanced because the effort is limited in scope. If such a project is successful, everyone benefits: The organization gains a solution to the problem, and both the practitioner and OD itself gain credibility.

However, a disadvantage exists in that success may be limited because of the many variables that influence business problems. Also, the organizational personnel may be impatient with the time required to obtain visible results; they may expect a "quick fix." If the project is unsuccessful, the practitioner may lose the opportunity to gain entry into other parts of the organization.

Control Through Action Research

In this situation the practitioner institutes a controlled experiment in which some aspect of the organization is changed and the impact is then monitored and evaluated. This type of activity is similar to the pilot project, but it is generally even more tightly controlled and limited in scope.

The associated advantages and disadvantages are also similar to those involved with the pilot-project approach. One additional disadvantage is that the practitioner may be viewed as a "researcher" who is separated from the mainstream of the organization.

Reduction of Organizational Pain

This approach is similar to concentration on a business problem except that "pain" is defined more broadly than is "problem." Organizational pain might include poor decision making or problem solving, the inability to obtain valid information from subordinates, excessive time spent in initiating and/or implementing OD efforts, the unwillingness of subordinates to take the initiative in directing their own activities, and so forth.

The advantages and disadvantages are similar to those associated with the business-problem approach, but an additional disadvantage is presented: The pain may be social or psychological in nature; therefore, improvement may be viewed as "soft" or "fuzzy" by personnel in other parts of the organization who are not actively involved in the effort. On the other hand, an additional advantage is that managers who receive help in reducing the kinds of pain illustrated can become intense supporters of the practitioner.

Involvement in an Imposed Change

This approach consists of becoming involved in a project or change that the organization has already mandated. Examples might include the promotion of a manager, a merger between two departments, the initiation of a new production process, or the starting of a new plant. This type of project might involve such interventions as a transition meeting, a merger meeting, or a new-plant start-up effort.

One particular advantage of this approach is that the need for change is already established. The change itself is the natural process employed in the intervention, which may make the organization more receptive to other OD activities. Similarly, the practitioner is seen as assisting in a natural and/or legitimate process and thus is considered to have a relevant, helpful function. The potential for success with such a project is relatively high, and the practitioner shares with others the responsibility for success.

However, certain potentially negative consequences should be considered. For example, the practitioner may be seen as a meddler. In addition, success in the project may be attributed to factors other than the OD interventions. Finally, the reasons for the change may not be consistent with OD values; therefore, the practitioner may be seen as hypocritical or unethical.

Association with the Influence Leader

This approach is similar to the power play except that the focus is on an individual rather than a group. The advantages and disadvantages are also similar. However, in this case success is determined by the relationship with one individual; and, if success is achieved, it may be extremely difficult for the practitioner to work in other areas of the organization in which the influence leader's work is envied or suspect.

Association with OD Support

With this approach activities are initiated in those parts of the organization that are already supportive of OD values and activity. Certain advantages are afforded by the fact that such projects can be initiated quickly and the potential for their success is high. Also, the employees involved feel a strong sense of ownership of these projects and perceive the practitioner as valuable.

In contrast, success with such projects may be viewed by personnel in other parts of the organization as merely perceived rather than real. Success may also accomplish little in the way of opening doors into other parts of the organization. In addition, the practitioner may be seen by the rest of the organization as just "one of those OD people." In fact, if the practitioner's support comes from a low-influence group, his or her own influence may actually diminish elsewhere.

Total-System Intervention

The objective of this approach is to affect all parts of the organization almost simultaneously. Such a project might be a new-plant start-up in which the practitioner or a team of practitioners is involved in every aspect of planning and implementation. Although some practitioners have proposed that a total-organization survey constitutes a total-system approach, the authors feel that such a definition is too ambitious in view of the limited number of variables considered in typical surveys.

The practitioner may benefit from this approach by being involved in every aspect of the organization, by having more control of the variables that affect his or her work, and by associating with the key managers and personnel. Moreover, if the project is successful, the practitioner gains great credibility and influence.

However, if the practitioner is not prepared for such an ambitious venture, the risk is great. Failure in this type of project has an extremely negative impact on the practitioner's credibility. In addition, few managers consider this approach to be a viable starting point for OD.

OVERCOMING FAILURE PATTERNS

Obviously, many OD efforts have failed or have achieved limited success. As a result of reviewing their own work and participating in discussions with other practitioners, the authors have identified certain types of practitioner failings that tend to precipitate failure in the effort itself.

- Failure to obtain and work through a contract (applicable to both external and internal practitioners);
- Failure to establish specific goals for efforts and interventions;
- Failure to demonstrate sufficient courage to confront the organization and key managers in particular;
- Failure to be willing to try something new;
- Failure to determine the identity of the real client;
- Failure to work with real organizational needs;
- Failure to implement genuine OD (by becoming involved in marketing rather than OD, for example);
- Failure to develop viable options;
- Failure to coordinate with the organization (by circumventing the thinking and readiness of its personnel);
- Failure to work with the organization as it is rather than as the practitioner would like it to be;
- Failure to measure or evaluate OD activities;
- Failure to plan for and avoid managerial abdication;
- Failure to solve problems (by becoming involved in "quick fixes");
- Failure to specify both short- and long-term goals for the effort;
- Failure to be honest about what needs to be done and why;
- Failure to determine whose needs are being met;

- Failure to plan for and build toward the client managers' ownership of the OD effort;
- Failure to escape entrapment in the "mystique" of OD, which leads to a distorted interpretation of the OD process; and
- Failure to tailor the effort to the jointly analyzed needs of the specific organization.

In reviewing these patterns a practitioner, particularly a relative newcomer to the field, might feel overwhelmed or discouraged. However, simply being aware that certain negative behavioral patterns are potentially damaging to OD efforts can help a practitioner to avoid such behaviors. In addition, the practitioner who conscientiously attends to the following activities may have greater success in overcoming failure patterns.

Building a Strategy

As discussed previously, one of the practitioner's primary responsibilities is to formulate a strategy. The systematic building of a strategy for specific activities and projects protects against failure by forcing the practitioner to consider and deal with such issues as developing a contract, establishing goals for the entire project as well as for the related interventions, and avoiding "quick fixes." In fact, a comprehensive strategy focuses attention on each of the failure patterns.

Establishing a Flow Diagram of Activities

Another practice that forces consideration of the issues involved in failure patterns is establishing a flow diagram covering all activities of the OD effort. A flow diagram provides an illustration of the ways in which the various interventions tie together and build on each other, the perceptions of the practitioner and the client personnel regarding progress at various points, and aspects related to the critical question of timing.

Engaging in Joint Planning with Prospective Clients

During proposal development and prior to the launching of a long-term effort, the practitioner should engage in joint planning with the prospective client. Without sufficient joint planning and exploration, the practitioner tends to proceed with a high risk of falling into at least one, if not several, of the failure patterns.

Incorporating Review and Evaluation Sessions

Of great help in avoiding failure patterns is the practice of incorporating into a contract a provision for periodic review and evaluation sessions. Such a meeting allows the practitioner and appropriate organizational participants and managers to examine the immediate activity and to ask such questions as the following:

- Are we on track?
- Are the expected results materializing?
- What feelings are we experiencing about our working relationship?

- What modifications or changes need to be made?
- Are any failure patterns beginning to appear in the project? If so, what can we do to eliminate them?

Using Consulting Teams

Directly or indirectly involving one or more fellow professionals enables the practitioner to be more aware of and sensitive to potential failure patterns. Such involvement generates more analysis, the sharing of different perceptions, the use of more specialized skills and experience in given interventions, and increased feedback and constructive confrontation.

In their own practice the authors involve at least two staff members in the development of every proposal. This procedure ensures that the appropriate questions are raised regarding failure patterns and that specific measures are planned to avoid them.

Participating in OD Activities

Frequently practitioners attempt to guide clients through OD activities that they themselves have not experienced as participants. Being a "disinterested observer" does not allow the practitioner to experience the dynamics and feelings of the "owner." A practitioner gains valuable experience in avoiding failure patterns when he or she participates in the application of the interventions outlined in this book. This firsthand experience can be invaluable in planning OD activities for others.

Ensuring Professional Development

To avoid failure in OD, practitioners must ensure their professional growth by continually updating their skills and conceptual frameworks. Failure patterns are avoided primarily by learning what they are and how others bypass them. A great deal of this information can be obtained by attending professional events such as those offered by University Associates, the OD Network, the Organization Development Division of the American Society for Training and Development (ASTD), the National Training Laboratories (NTL) Institute, or local OD groups. Participation in developmental seminars and laboratories on such subjects as human interaction, consulting skills, and conflict resolution may provide insights into patterns of success as well as patterns of failure. Such experiences are invaluable in helping the practitioner to understand his or her effect on others.

Still another source of professional development is the practitioner's association with other professionals on individual projects. This association generates new ideas, perspectives, and experiences that have a positive impact on avoidance of failure patterns.

Resting and Relaxing

Successful OD activities can be and generally are physically and emotionally draining. The authors' personal experiences and those of others clearly demonstrate that we are in a field that involves a high level of burnout. Heavy schedules, airplane and automobile travel, hotel living, erratic sleeping patterns, and simultaneously conducted projects for several different clients all have an impact on effective planning and execution. Under these conditions the practitioner runs the risk of doing the same things over and over again without sufficient preparation, skipping essential analytical activity, and losing his or her professional advantage.

Contemporary literature is replete with good advice on coping with stress in today's world.[2] The practitioner is advised to become familiar with different approaches to stress management and to seek periods of rest and relaxation away from OD activity and other stress. Without this time to clear the mind and to refresh the body and spirit, the probability of failure is greatly increased.

---

[2]See, for example, J.D. Adams, *Understanding and Managing Stress: A Workbook in Changing Life Styles.* San Diego, CA: University Associates, 1980.

PART II
INTERVENTION DESIGNS

Now that the authors' practice theories have been developed, the step-by-step implementation of various interventions may be presented. The authors recognize, of course, that the experience of others may differ from their own and that in an expanding field such as OD one never achieves the "last word" in technology. Nevertheless, they believe that the reader will benefit from the information included in these intervention designs and will be able to use this information to enhance his or her own practice.

GENERAL INTRODUCTION TO THE INTERVENTIONS

The designs are grouped into chapters as follows:

1. Chapter 5, which consists of interventions that focus on the basic unit in all organizations, *natural work groups;*
2. Chapter 6, which includes interventions with a broader focus directed toward total systems and *organizational structures;* and
3. Chapter 7, which presents interventions that involve *specific training* that complements the designs in the two preceding chapters.

As the practitioner assists clients in analyzing organizational needs according to the model of OD developed in Chapter 2, the need for specific interventions in the sociosystem, the process system, and/or the technosystem will become apparent. The specific intervention that is most appropriate in a given situation depends, of course, on the results of the joint analysis. Therefore, the authors have chosen an intervention format that is comprehensive enough to meet the practitioner's needs and yet understandable to the client.

FORMAT

Each intervention design consists of the following three components:

1. The *overview,* which is useful in marketing and contracting efforts and which provides a general outline of the intervention as well as answers to the questions that clients most frequently ask;

2. The *action sequence,* which is useful in both marketing and on-site consulting and which supplies a step-by-step summary of implementation; and
3. The *operating procedure,* which is useful in planning and facilitating the intervention process and which provides a detailed explanation of each step as outlined in the action sequence, including related suggestions, cautions, explanations, and rationales.

Overview

The overview initially presents the primary *objectives* of the intervention and then its related *focus,* which identifies specific task, maintenance, or interpersonal-process factors that are typically present within a given participating group. The *target group* for which the intervention was designed is then identified, along with the typical *group size* and the optimal *setting* for the intervention. The practitioner and client are then given some idea of the *duration* of the intervention, which, of course, is contingent on such factors as the size of the target group, its current level of development, whether this is its first experience with the process in question, and so forth.

A brief description of the *methods* to be employed is then provided, coupled with the *rationale for methods.* The *probable content* is also discussed in terms of the amount of time required for specific phases of the intervention.

The nature of the need for third-party *practitioner involvement,* whether from inside or outside the parent organization, is clarified next. Finally, the *time sequence* of the intervention is specified with regard to its use in a multiphased OD strategy or effort.

The reader should note that when one of these categories is not relevant to a particular intervention, it has been omitted.

Action Sequence

This step-by-step summary provides a specific sequence of events. Although some readers may feel that following such a sequence might detract from the benefits of spontaneity, creativity, and flexibility in meeting emerging needs, the authors have not found this to be the case. Every successful OD practitioner eventually learns to trust his or her instincts regarding deviations from a given agenda. Beneficial deviations are to be expected and are encouraged. However, experience indicates that certain specific events generally lead to and support others in a complementary fashion if they are appropriately sequenced. Although the order of some of the events listed as taking place in the middle of an intervention is sometimes not critical, the authors have discovered that the beginning and final events may be ignored only at a price.

Operating Procedure

The third component of each intervention design contains detailed information shared from numerous experiences with the process in question. Too often the interventions presented in OD literature are outlined so generally that the practitioner is left to guess at the specifics of facilitating the required process steps; even when the steps are outlined sufficiently, usually there is no concrete explanation for them coupled with related hints or cautions born of experience. Thus, the authors have attempted to correct this deficiency by supplying such information.

NATURAL WORK GROUPS

The fundamental unit in organizational society from an OD standpoint is the *natural work group*, which consists of co-workers who share a common leader and a clear unit mission or purpose that requires a degree of interaction born of interdependence. In the larger organizational context, a major system consists of connected work groups that share a common mission or purpose.

Some organizations label these groups "teams"; but, as discussed in Chapter 1, teamwork and related collaborative behavior may or may not in fact exist within a group that is to be the subject of an OD intervention. Indeed, one of the felt needs of such a group may be to improve the level of cooperation among members. Because member interaction is generally the key to a natural work group's current level of effectiveness, the interventions developed in this chapter relate primarily to the dynamics and factors associated with such interaction: problem solving, decision making, planning and establishing priorities, communicating, role clarification, and conflict resolution.

OWNERSHIP AND COMMITMENT

The authors' rationale for the intervention designs and operating recommendations presented in this chapter is based on group ownership and commitment: *The best answers to questions regarding a group's effectiveness generally lie within the group itself.* This rationale evolves from the premise that, given an opportunity and some process tools, most members of a group are collectively capable of analyzing and solving their own relationship and task problems. The tools required are vehicles for accomplishing the following:

- Gathering valid data about how the members are working together;
- Identifying priority issues reflected in these data; and
- Focusing group energy on improving situations over which the group has some control.

Although this practice theory does not mean that the practitioner should never offer advice regarding specific problems or solutions, it does place primary emphasis on his or her skills as a group-process facilitator.

INTERVENTION CATEGORIES

The designs that follow are grouped in accordance with the typical life cycle of a natural work group.

1. Interventions that have to do with the beginnings of either a totally new group of co-workers or an ongoing group that is acquiring a new leader:
   - New-Team Start-Up
   - Transition Planning

2. An intervention that is associated with the development or renewal of a natural work group's ongoing effectiveness:
   - Team Building

3. Interventions that are concerned with crucial intergroup relationships:
   - Multigroup Mirror
   - Issue Census
   - Intergroup Team Building

NEW-TEAM START-UP
OVERVIEW

Objectives
- To accelerate the processes by which individual group members coordinate their efforts and become an efficient and effective team
- To articulate and begin to practice the desired norms for the team's interaction

Focus

Task
- Collective vision of the team's mission
- Individual roles and related responsibilities
- Coordination of plans and strategies
- Definition of the team's effectiveness
- Plans for evaluating the team's effectiveness

Interpersonal Process
- Membership issues
- Desired norms regarding the feedback process, interpersonal and role conflicts, and conflict-resolution methods

Target Group
- A newly formed group (matrix organization, project group, new-company start-up, and so forth)

Group Size
- All members of the immediate work group (supervisor and subordinates)

Setting
- A comfortable facility in which the participants can be free from routine activities and distractions

Duration
- Two and one-half to four days, depending on the ambiguity and complexity of the team's mission

Methods
- The practitioner and the key members of the group meet to clarify expected outcomes and to plan the program agenda.
- The group works as a whole; when appropriate, subgroups are formed to negotiate specific coordinating procedures.
- As the group works on defining the team's mission, member roles, and operating procedures, the practitioner reports observations and initiates discussion about membership and norms as they relate to the team's effectiveness.

Rationale for Methods
- An atmosphere is established for dealing openly with team-membership issues.
- The group members are provided with an opportunity to work together on understanding their mission, roles, and interacting processes.
- The group members observe each other in various situations.
- The group members share their ideas and experiences and develop short-term plans for achieving the needed results.

Probable Content

- Approximately one day for the planning session
- One-half to one day for getting acquainted and for analyzing the team's mission as well as what that mission means in relation to other company missions and activities
- One-half to one day for determining questions and concerns about the team's mission and goals, summarizing key issues, and analyzing responsibilities and roles
- One-half to one day for action planning with regard to task accomplishments and for evaluating the intervention

Practitioner Involvement

- Serves as co-facilitator with the group leader (the group leader outlines tasks and facilitates discussion)
- Functions primarily as a clarifier of agenda, a process observer, and an interviewer

Time Relevance

- The first step for individuals who are forming a team to accomplish their goals
- Followed by a session three to six months later to review progress and to improve the team's norms and operating procedures

NEW-TEAM START-UP
ACTION SEQUENCE

1

Planning Session

- Developing a contract
- Sharing and clarifying general session goals and expectations
- Planning the meeting agenda

2

Getting-Acquainted Process

- Sharing aspects of personal history, characteristics, and values
- Responding to related questions

3

Establishment of Mission and Goals

- Developing or reaffirming the group mission
- Identifying team goals and general objectives

4

Determination of Questions and Concerns

- Surfacing specific questions and concerns
- Listing related hopes, expectations, and/or recommendations

5

Issue Summary

- Integrating key issues
- Developing key-issue summary

6

Preliminary Role Negotiation

- As appropriate, identifying and clarifying specific roles within the team
- Discussing roles

7

Action Planning

- Identifying specific objectives requiring follow-through
- Developing related plans for action

8

Evaluation

- Evaluating group accomplishments from a process standpoint
- Discussing group norms observed/felt during the intervention

NEW-TEAM START-UP
OPERATING PROCEDURE

A new-team start-up intervention is aimed at the development of a group that is either convening for the first time, whether on a permanent or an ad-hoc basis, or undergoing such a radical change in composition or direction (such as when one or more new managers are added) that for all practical purposes it is a new group.

When dealing with a brand-new group, the procedure is different from that which is followed when most of the members remain together from a previous team. (The case of a simple changeover in team leader is covered in the intervention package entitled "Transition Planning" in this chapter.) An entirely new group typically is formed when a major reorganization has taken place or is taking place, when a new plant or other structure is about to be opened, or in a matrix organization* when a temporary ad-hoc task force is being created.

1. *Planning Session*

   The planning session takes place some time prior to the actual working session. Its basic purpose is to ensure that the practitioner and the key members of the group have developed at least a verbal contract covering the objectives and content of the intervention.

   Planning consists of jointly determining the meeting agenda, specific activities to be used, and communications to participants. In addition, the practitioner and the key group members should share expectations.

2. *Getting-Acquainted Process*

   This is a key "unfreezing" event aimed at beginning the session while establishing an atmosphere that is relatively open and caring at the interpersonal level. The authors have found that the best approach is simply to ask each member of the group to share information about himself or herself. For example, the following incomplete sentences can be distributed and the participants can be asked to work individually for a few minutes to write completions to be shared with the rest of the group.

   - As far as work is concerned, I was reared to believe...
   - One of the most influential people in my life (other than my parents) has been _____ because...
   - The thing that I remember most about what I was like as a teenager is...
   - In my leisure time I enjoy...
   - One thing that I would like to improve about myself is...
   - One of the biggest disappointments that I have had to deal with is...
   - Although I seldom talk about it, I am proud of...
   - The qualities that I particularly value in co-workers are...

---

*See S.M. Davis, "Matrix: Filling the Gap Between Theory and Practice," in W.W. Burke (Ed.), *The Cutting Edge: Current Theory and Practice in Organization Development.* San Diego, CA: University Associates, 1978.

- It frankly disturbs me when people at work...
- If I had the money, I would...
- When I retire I hope that the organization remembers me as...
- To become a more effective person, I am working on...

It is helpful to tell the participants that they need not respond to all of these items unless they so desire. This practice avoids any undue discomfort that the participants may feel about sharing certain information at this early stage. In addition, it is usually helpful if the practitioner shares personal information with the group, thereby setting the stage for the participants and establishing his or her membership in the group.

The participants should be encouraged to relax and take whatever time they need in sharing information. After each participant has finished sharing, the practitioner inquires about questions that the other group members might want to ask.

Finally, to provide a transition into subsequent events, the practitioner asks the participants to list the general themes that arose during the data sharing and to build on these in terms of the following question: "What norms would we like to see operate during this session in order to derive the greatest benefit?"

3. Establishment of Mission and Goals

It is important at this stage to spend some time either developing or reaffirming a statement of the team's "mission" or reason for existing in the organization. Although many group members may temporarily find themselves in a quandary over semantics, it is well worth the effort to facilitate their writing a statement that clearly sets forth the objectives of their team. The mission statement should not be detailed and lengthy, however; it should remain intentionally general and no longer than three sentences.

Then the participants are asked to develop a list of goals that are consistent with and supportive of the mission statement. Here again brevity and generality are important so that the group does not become involved in unproductive discussion at this early point. The important thing is to force the group to focus on its core purpose and thus generate data and surface issues with which it will need to deal both now and later in order to become an effective team.

4. Determination of Questions and Concerns

The participants are asked to form subgroups of approximately three to five each, depending on the size of the total group. Each subgroup's task is to use the mission and goal data developed in the previous step as a base and to discuss and then record on newsprint any questions and concerns that the members may have about these data.

A second task for each subgroup is to establish recommendations regarding ways to deal with its questions and concerns. However, if the practitioner feels that the subgroups are not ready for this second task, it may be delayed until the action-planning stage.

The rationale for this step is as follows: Newly reorganizing groups invariably have questions and concerns about old issues and about whether or not they may expect relief from these issues as a result of the change. Completely new groups also will have generated concerns during the discussion involved in step 3. In either case, these thoughts and feelings need to be surfaced.

5. *Issue Summary*

At this point the subgroups report their data, posting this information on the wall for reference, and respond to questions for clarification only. While listening to these reports, the practitioner records on newsprint the items that he or she feels are representative of key issues. Then the participants are asked to name other key issues that they have identified as a result of integrating data from all subgroups, and these responses are also recorded on newsprint. This summary list of key issues serves as a discussion and planning agenda for the balance of the session.

Care should be taken to encourage candid reactions to the practitioner's list, however, to ensure that the resulting agenda is owned by the group. Otherwise, the "outsider's" perceptions of key issues may prevail unchallenged and may lead to a loss of ownership and commitment. If the practitioner senses strong questioning of or negative reaction to his or her list, the best thing to do is to discard this list and to use the participants' responses exclusively. However, the authors' usual experience is that the practitioner's preliminary list saves considerable time spent in consolidating and avoids tendencies to duplicate items or to word them in terms that are ambiguous or that do not lend themselves to effective action planning. This is particularly true with groups whose members have relatively weak verbal skills.

6. *Preliminary Role Negotiation*

In most new-team start-up sessions, one of the key issues in the list developed in step 5 is that of role ambiguity or confusion. This is to be expected because newly forming relationships almost invariably involve the need to clarify individual perceptions and expectations about roles.

If this is the case, one of the most productive steps in this intervention process is to identify several key roles and to focus on them individually by clarifying the following information:*

- What the incumbent's role definition is;
- What the incumbent's expectations are regarding other specific members of the team with whom he or she will interact;
- What the other specific members' reactions to the incumbent's definition and expectations are; and
- What specific matters require a negotiated agreement to ensure that collaborative relationships are established or continue, as the situation dictates.

7. *Action Planning*

Whether or not role negotiation occurs in the previous step, the group should now be ready to develop a list of action items required to take advantage of all of the data generated thus far. As is typically the case with any action plan, each item thus identified should be the focus of a discussion led by the practitioner. As a result of this discussion, the following information should be recorded for the team's retention:

---

*See the intervention package entitled "Role Development" in Chapter 6 for further details and process suggestions for this step.

- The identity of the action item;
- The related objective;
- The specific ways in which the objective will be achieved;
- The members who will be involved, including the individual who will coordinate follow-up meetings; and
- The dates by which specific milestones as well as the final objective will be accomplished.

With certain groups the practitioner may need to exert special effort to keep the discussion focused on the task at hand, to suggest optional steps for the group members to consider as parts of their plan, and to insist that each of the previously mentioned types of information be recorded. Failing to exert this effort may result in little or no follow-through on the part of group members.

An alternative approach to this process is to make certain that all action items have been finalized and posted in order of development before establishing a deadline for each. This practice ensures prioritization and appropriate sequencing and prevents the group from setting too many objectives for a given follow-through period. When impossible numbers of objectives are set, the group can become discouraged and abandon the project because of failure to meet deadlines.

8. *Evaluation*

Before the group is dismissed, the practitioner should insist that the members spend a few minutes evaluating their accomplishments from a *process* standpoint. Questions such as the following can be asked:

- How well do you think that you worked together during this session?
- What were the "highs" and "lows" of your session?
- What could you have done to overcome the "lows"?
- What have you learned about your tendencies as a group?
- How can you profit from your learnings?

The practitioner may choose to add his or her own observations about the group's process behavior. One way to lead into these personal observations is to ask whether the participants have any questions about the session.

The practitioner may also wish to ask each participant to rate each of the following on a scale of 1 to 10:

- How open and honest were we?
- Were the "right" issues surfaced and dealt with?
- How would you rate the quality of the action plans?
- What is your level of optimism regarding follow-through?
- How helpful was the consultant?
- How would you rate the overall session?

These data may be posted and discussed by the group, thus negating the tendency for some individuals to leave with erroneous impressions of the group's feelings about its work and the session.

TRANSITION PLANNING
OVERVIEW

Objectives
- To provide an opportunity for a work group to analyze the impact of and plan its adjustment to a new supervisor
- To give a newly appointed work-group leader an opportunity to become familiar with group activities, goals, and individual resources
- To allow both the incoming leader and the work-group members to share and examine working styles and preferred task methods

Focus

Task
- Group goals, tasks, methods, and priorities
- Group structure and operating procedure
- Individual roles and contributions to group performance
- Incoming supervisor's experience, goals, and priorities
- Coordination of the incoming supervisor's preferences with individual and group preferences

Interpersonal Process
- Apprehensions of the group and the incoming supervisor
- Trust, openness, and risk taking
- Communication and decision-making styles
- Managerial styles
- Role conflict and ambiguity
- Feedback processes
- Resistance to change

Target Group
- A transition work group (incoming supervisor, outgoing supervisor, and subordinates)

Group Size
- The size of the work group involved in the leadership transition

Setting
- On site for data collection
- Off site preferable for meetings to provide an uninterrupted setting and to reinforce neutral, future-oriented planning

Duration
- Approximately four to five days, depending on group size and data-collection methods

| **Methods** | • The practitioner and the potential participants meet to clarify the purpose of the forthcoming transition meetings and to obtain commitments for necessary preparation/follow-up activity. |

• Prior to the actual transition meetings, data are collected from each team member, including the incoming supervisor, regarding perceptions of key questions and concerns, apprehensions about activities and roles, and estimates of key strengths and weaknesses in the work group.

• Individual replies are compiled into a handout.

• In the first transition meeting, which involves the incoming and outgoing supervisors and all work-group members, group goals and activities are reviewed and clarified, management styles are discussed, and the interview data published in the handout are analyzed.

• On the following day, a second meeting is held at which the incoming supervisor and the work-group members examine concerns that arose from the previous day's meeting or that have not yet been discussed. In addition, roles are clarified and action plans are developed to deal with problems regarding changing roles, management style, and work-group goals and activities.

Rationale for Methods

• All participants are afforded the opportunity to analyze the group's performance and resource utilization.

• Collection and dissemination of data accelerate the process of identifying and dealing with group concerns.

• Awareness is heightened regarding teamwork needs in a significantly changing situation.

• The group members receive information about the status of current projects and activities.

• The new supervisor quickly learns about work-role requirements and relationships.

• A meaningful, task-oriented opportunity is provided for mutual adjustments of group practice and managerial style.

• The new supervisor as well as the group members experience less stress in making adjustments in assignments.

• Teamwork is enhanced by the opportunity for group members and the incoming supervisor to get to know one another and to collaborate on clarification of goals and objectives.

Probable Content

• One day of prework to establish a contract, plan the transition meeting, and determine specifics regarding data collection

• One or more days of data collection

• One day of discussing and evaluating current operations, management styles, and the data collected

• One day of analyzing concerns, developing task-related plans, clarifying roles, and evaluating the intervention

Practitioner Involvement

• Imperative that an internal or external practitioner facilitate prework, data collection, discussion, analysis, and planning

• Follow-up meetings to be handled either by the incoming supervisor or by the practitioner

Time Relevance

• Especially suitable for a group that is new to OD (that is, as an initial intervention)

• Can also be used for more in-depth analysis of work-style preferences as well as task issues with a group that has previously participated in skill-building interventions or other OD activities

• Followed by sessions at later dates to review progress

TRANSITION PLANNING
ACTION SEQUENCE

1

Prework Session
(All Participants)

- Establishing a contract
- Clarifying purposes, format, and content
- Determining data-collection items and process

2

Data Collection

- Gathering information from individuals (via questionnaires, interviews, or tape-recorded discussions)
- Compiling information into handouts

3

Operations Review
(All Participants)

- Clarifying current goals and objectives as well as current projects and activities

4

Management-Style Review
(All Participants)

- Identifying similarities and possible differences in the supervisors' leadership styles

5

Data Feedback and Analysis
(All Participants)

- Disclosing, clarifying, and analyzing data regarding concerns about the change

6

Issue Census
(New Team)

- Identifying key issues
- Developing plans to deal with key issues

7

Role Clarification
(New Team)

- Redefining/reaffirming roles
- Reviewing goals and objectives to establish trade-offs between old ones and new ones

8

Evaluation
(New Team)

- Assessing the meeting
- Planning follow-up

TRANSITION PLANNING
OPERATING PROCEDURE

The movement of supervisors in and out of existing managerial positions is a fact of organizational life. When one supervisor replaces another, the result is often an extended period of confusion, reduced communication, and lowered output as members of the work unit adjust to the change. Such uncertainty is normal and is to be expected when managerial changes are made. However, if the new supervisor does not deal quickly and effectively with this uncertainty, it is highly probable that subordinates will begin to speculate about their future. In this kind of situation, often the levels of productivity and quality decrease, nonproductive communication increases, and work on major projects either slows down or is discontinued. Transition planning represents an alternative approach that safeguards against these negative consequences.

1. *Prework Session (All Participants)*

   This session normally takes place at least two weeks prior to the first transition-meeting date. It is attended by the outgoing and incoming supervisors as well as all members of the work group. Its basic purpose is to establish a contract and to reach a consensus regarding the purpose, format, and content of the intervention. Because data are to be collected in advance of the meeting, at this time the participants should also develop the questions to be used to obtain these data. Specific types of data collected depend on the nature of the work unit. Sample questions for the unit members include the following:

   - What concerns do you have about the fact that your current supervisor is leaving the unit?
   - What aspects of the outgoing supervisor's leadership style have been particularly helpful to you?
   - What are the major objectives that should be accomplished by this unit in the coming months?

   The outgoing supervisor might be asked the following questions:

   - What concerns do you have about leaving this work unit?
   - To what extent do you feel that this work unit has accomplished the goals that have been set for it?

   Questions for the incoming supervisor might include the following:

   - What concerns do you have about joining this particular work unit?
   - What can the individual unit members do to be of help to you?

   At this session the participants must also decide how the data are to be collected; common alternatives include questionnaires, interviews, and tape-recorded discussions. Experience demonstrates that in-depth interviews are particularly helpful in identifying the basic issues that are likely to have an effect on the transition.

2. *Data Collection*

   Through questionnaires, interviews, or tape-recorded discussions, answers are obtained for the questions developed during the prework session. These data should be collected far enough in advance of the first transition meeting to be compiled and made available to all participants at that meeting, but not so far in advance that they become obsolete. It is recommended that all information be recorded as accurately as possible and not be summarized or otherwise edited; the group itself can later distill from these data the key issues and concerns. Also, the sources of specific comments should not be listed in the handouts in which these data are published.

3. *Operations Review (All Participants)*

This phase initiates the first actual transition meeting. All parties should be present, including the outgoing and incoming supervisors. The practitioner should help the participants to surface and discuss the goals and objectives that are currently being pursued by the group in accordance with its mission. Current projects, key events, and activities should be summarized and explained by members of the unit; during this process the incoming supervisor should be allowed to ask questions and elicit reactions from the entire group, including the outgoing supervisor. The basic purpose of this step is to apprise the new supervisor of key priorities, goals, and related activities.

4. *Management-Style Review (All Participants)*

This step represents another phase of the first transition meeting. The outgoing and incoming supervisors outline their respective managerial or leadership styles, employing whatever models or vehicles that they find useful. The purpose of this process is not to critique these styles, but to give the members of the work unit an opportunity to hear the leaders' expressions of their self-images concerning operating style, thus facilitating comparisons, answering questions, and resolving ambiguities. The two supervisors should be informed in advance of this segment so that they can think through their presentations.

5. *Data Feedback and Analysis (All Participants)*

In the final phase of the first transition meeting, handouts consisting of the data collected during step 2 are distributed. An opportunity is provided for clarification, with the outgoing supervisor serving as a source of information regarding the possible meaning or significance of various data.

6. *Issue Census (New Team)*

This step begins the second transition meeting, which is attended by the members of the work unit and their new supervisor. The data collected earlier serve as the basis for this meeting.

All participants, including the new supervisor, are assembled into subgroups to identify key issues reflected in the data and to explore any concerns that they may have regarding the fate of various activities and objectives that originated with the outgoing supervisor. The resulting lists of important items are shared among subgroups, and a master list of priority issues is developed. The entire unit then develops specific plans to deal with those issues requiring action. The new supervisor can commit himself or herself to specific behaviors believed to be helpful to the unit and, insofar as is possible, can clarify his or her position on matters not requiring specific action. This phase also provides an opportunity for the team to engage in a more in-depth analysis of the new supervisor's style and to develop plans and/or commitments to ensure a productive relationship between supervisor and subordinates.

7. Role Clarification (New Team)

At this point in the second transition meeting, the new team discusses the roles to be played in the work group, outlining those of both subordinates and supervisor that are believed to be the most helpful to the group in achieving its objectives. The team also outlines ways in which these roles might change in the future and develops appropriate plans to ensure flexibility and responsiveness to changing needs.

The goals and objectives presented in step 3 are reviewed in light of the team's conclusions about its key roles as well as the plans developed in step 6. After any necessary or appropriate changes have been specified, plans are established to facilitate the accomplishment of all goals. This process both reaffirms old objectives and facilitates trade-offs between old ones and new ones.

8. Evaluation (New Team)

A formal evaluation of the second transition meeting is conducted, and plans are developed to ensure follow-up and action regarding the decisions made during this meeting. Dates are set to review the progress of the unit.

TEAM BUILDING
OVERVIEW

Objectives
- To examine and improve the work group's effectiveness
- To provide an opportunity for the group as a whole to analyze its functioning, performance, strengths, and weaknesses
- To identify problem areas of team behavior and corrective actions to be taken
- To allow the group to plan for its future via follow-up

Focus

Task
- Group performance
- Individual contributions to performance and overall coordination
- Group goals, long- and short-range strategies, and goal-setting processes
- Specific plans for individuals in connection with group roles
- Group composition, structure, operating procedures, and efficiency

Interpersonal Process/Group Maintenance
- Group identity and individual allegiance
- Group norms and culture
- Feedback processes
- Group-process roles
- Conflict-resolution methods
- Capabilities for coping
- Problem ownership
- Supervisor/subordinate relationships
- Subgroups and coalitions
- Interpersonal and role conflict
- Other interpersonal-process elements (trust, openness, and so forth)

Target Group
- A natural work group (supervisor and subordinates)

Group Size
- All members of the work group

Setting
- On site for the contract session, prework session, and interviews
- Off site for the team-building meeting

Duration
- Approximately five days, depending on group size

Methods	• The practitioner and the work-group leader meet to establish a contract, clarify expectations, and plan the intervention.

- Ten to twenty questions pertaining to the group's specific concerns are developed by the group members with the assistance of the practitioner.
- Each group member is interviewed separately by the practitioner and provides confidential replies to the questions previously developed.
- All replies to each question are compiled into a handout.
- Copies of the handout are distributed to group members immediately prior to the team-building meeting.
- The handout data are analyzed by the group; problems are identified, defined, and ranked according to importance.
- Action plans are developed to deal with each problem.

Rationale for Methods

- This process provides a setting for a candid, realistic self-appraisal of group functions and member interactions; the supervisor and subordinates give feedback to each other and share perceptions of their roles in relation to the total group's operation.
- Dealing with anonymous, topic-related data permits problem-centered rather than person-centered analysis.
- The supervisor is provided an opportunity to model the type of behavior preferred for effective team efforts.
- Group members can best uncover new and/or subtle problems and develop effective resolutions by sharing ideas, relating experiences, and using others' approaches when appropriate.
- Teamwork is enhanced when group members become better acquainted, especially in terms of work-style preferences and in the context of particular work conditions and pressures.

Probable Content

- One day for the contract session
- One-half day for the prework session
- One or more days of individual interviews, depending on the number of participants (two hours per interview)
- Two days for the team-building meeting: discussion and interpretation of interview data for approximately 50 percent of the time, with the remainder focused on the development of action plans for solving problems and evaluation of the intervention

Practitioner Involvement

- Imperative that an external practitioner be involved
- Can be helpful in follow-up or repeat sessions

Time Relevance

- Usually not the first step for a group unless its members are reasonably familiar with teamwork concepts, problems, and practices
- Useful as an early step for a top-level group in the organization (prior to active, lower-level interventions)
- Followed by a session three to nine months later to evaluate progress on action plans

TEAM BUILDING
ACTION SEQUENCE

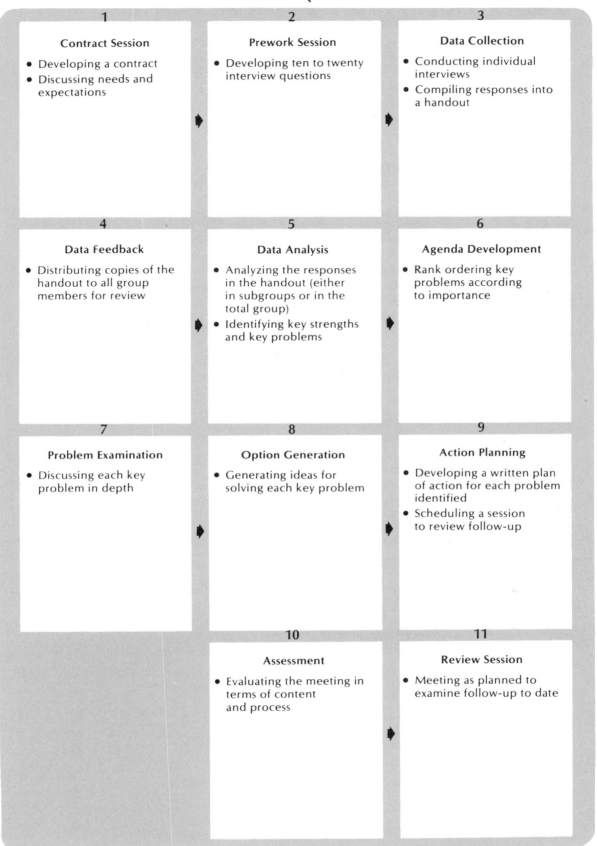

1

Contract Session

- Developing a contract
- Discussing needs and expectations

2

Prework Session

- Developing ten to twenty interview questions

3

Data Collection

- Conducting individual interviews
- Compiling responses into a handout

4

Data Feedback

- Distributing copies of the handout to all group members for review

5

Data Analysis

- Analyzing the responses in the handout (either in subgroups or in the total group)
- Identifying key strengths and key problems

6

Agenda Development

- Rank ordering key problems according to importance

7

Problem Examination

- Discussing each key problem in depth

8

Option Generation

- Generating ideas for solving each key problem

9

Action Planning

- Developing a written plan of action for each problem identified
- Scheduling a session to review follow-up

10

Assessment

- Evaluating the meeting in terms of content and process

11

Review Session

- Meeting as planned to examine follow-up to date

TEAM BUILDING
OPERATING PROCEDURE

1. *Contract Session*

   The contract session is critical; it establishes the working relationship between client and practitioner for the entire intervention. During the session the work-group leader surfaces needs, answers the practitioner's questions, raises any concerns about the content and format of the team-building meeting, and so forth. To avoid the development of any misunderstandings in the future, both parties express their expectations. The practitioner outlines the action sequence, making suggestions regarding logistics, timing, and facilities. In addition, arrangements for handling data are made and financial matters are finalized. Any of these details may be recorded in the form of a contract and/or meeting minutes.

2. *Prework Session*

   The primary purpose of this event is to involve as many of the intervention participants as possible in an exchange of information about the upcoming team-building meeting. The practitioner starts the session by eliciting questions from the group as a guide for an overview presentation about the upcoming meeting. Then all group members are encouraged to participate in a discussion aimed at developing specific questions for subsequent individual interviews. If desired, the practitioner may distribute a list of suggested interview questions to be used as a starting point; or the participants may be asked simply to generate questions about such key areas of team effectiveness as goals and priorities, work load, role clarity, decision making, problem solving, communications, conflict management, interpersonal competence and impact, and so forth. In either case, the practitioner should help the group members to develop ownership of the data to be gathered.

3. *Data Collection*

   The practitioner interviews each member of the work group, employing the questions developed in step 2. Although no attempt should be made to identify specific data with the person being interviewed, neither should guarantees of anonymity be made. The rationale for this approach is that the information collected should be recorded as accurately as possible without editing by the practitioner, and idiosyncrasies of expression or other comments may reveal identities. Thus, those being interviewed should not be pushed to disclose information that they are unwilling to deal with in the upcoming meeting; on the other hand, neither should the practitioner encourage the group members to mention information in so general, superficial, or nonspecific a manner as to render it obscure or useless.

   After all data have been collected, they should be compiled into a handout; each response to a given question should be clearly denoted, and all pages should be numbered for ease in reference.

4. *Data Feedback*

   To allow each group member ample time to read the data at his or her own pace, the practitioner should distribute copies of the handout to take home and review the night before the off-site meeting. However, this material should not be distributed until the group members are ready to leave their offices the day before the meeting; otherwise, they might engage in counterproductive, premature exchanges that the practitioner cannot monitor.

5. *Data Analysis*

This event takes place early during the actual off-site meeting. It is usually preceded by appropriate introductory remarks made by the group leader. In addition, the practitioner should provide a short introduction that is tailored to group needs. It is most useful to set a tone and climate of openness, for example, by discussing mutual expectations and related norms of behavior for achieving these expectations. Generally this is best accomplished by simply asking the group members to share their goals for the meeting and to identify what they must do to reach these goals. The resulting participant comments should be posted for all to see during the meeting. This procedure provides an initial set of expectation data that may be compared to actual accomplishments at the end of the meeting.

The participants are then asked to identify both key strengths and key problems by analyzing the data in the handout. To complete this task, the participants work either as a total group or in subgroups, depending on which approach the practitioner deems more useful.

6. *Agenda Development*

Using the data generated during the previous phase, the practitioner leads the group in a process designed to build a discussion agenda for in-depth treatment of key problems. If, for example, the group was assembled into subgroups in step 5, at this time the total group compares the subgroup results and notes similarities and overlaps; if all participants worked together in step 5, the group decisions regarding major issues of concern are now posted. In either case the group is helped to rank order all key problems according to importance for subsequent discussion.

7. *Problem Examination*

During this phase it is important that the group engage in a discussion that enables it to separate cause from symptom; each specific problem identified in step 5 and rank ordered in step 6 must be defined in sufficient detail to ensure that subsequent planning addresses the source of the matter rather than its surface manifestations. This type of discussion requires skillful facilitating on the part of the practitioner, who must provide sufficient focus and direction to help the group to deal with troublesome or potentially threatening issues. The participants should not be permitted to generate solutions at this point; if they are allowed to do so, they might engage in a superficial and relatively ineffective discussion about solving the less-difficult problems in an attempt to avoid the more-difficult ones.*

Thorough examination of each of the group's major problems is essential to team building, even though temporary tensions may develop and have to be worked

---

*Practitioners are occasionally challenged as to the need for an "outsider" to facilitate a team-building meeting. After participating in this particular discussion as well as subsequent events, groups often admit that they would have floundered without outside assistance.

through. Insufficient examination results in relatively weak and ineffective planning as well as little energy for change.

8. *Option Generation*

In this step the group generates a list of optional ideas for resolving the areas of concern that have been discussed. Typically this phase should begin the second day of the meeting, although in some cases the participants' needs and level of involvement may indicate that solutions should be listed while the nature of each problem is fresh on their minds. One approach is to list solution suggestions as they emerge during the previous step with the intention of using them at this time, thus avoiding the participants' frustration at being denied the opportunity to express solutions while examining problems.

9. *Action Planning*

At this point the group develops a written plan of action for each key problem, addressing the following questions:

- What is to be done to solve the problem?
- How will it be done?
- Who will be involved and/or responsible?
- When will it be completed?

This document thus becomes a guideline for effecting appropriate changes in accordance with the participants' wishes; after the meeting copies are prepared and distributed to all participants. A review session is scheduled for a time deemed appropriate by the group.

10. *Assessment*

To conclude the meeting, the practitioner assists the participants in evaluating the team-building process in terms of their original expectations and other criteria deemed appropriate. For example, the following questions can be asked:

- Did we discuss the right issues?
- What was the quality of openness?
- How would you rate the action plans?
- How optimistic are you about follow-through?
- Do you have any feedback for the consultant?
- How would you rate the overall session?

Further commentary may be elicited if the climate suggests that it would be beneficial, but redundant or superficial testimonials should not be forced. It is important, however, that the participants leave with a definite understanding of the group's reaction to the experience. They may also want to discuss back-home issues such as how to handle subordinates' inquiries about the experience. If so, these issues should be dealt with before dismissing the group.

11. *Review Session*

A review session is usually held three to nine months after the initial experience, depending on the nature of the action plans. The agenda for this event is an itemized evaluation of follow-through on actions planned. Each item is addressed separately via such questions as the following:

- How do we rate our follow-up to date?
- Have we accomplished our goals? If not, why?
- What further commitments or resources are required to ensure success?
- What new issues have developed since our last session? What should be done about them?

MULTIGROUP MIRROR
OVERVIEW

Objectives
- To examine the interactions of three or more interdependent work groups, with particular emphasis on improving the effectiveness of the group that is designated as the "host" or principal group
- To provide an opportunity for these groups to disclose perceptions of each other in terms of contributions to one another's effectiveness, impact on overall effectiveness, individual and mutual goals, and specific actions that occur in each area, with special attention directed toward the principal group
- To identify problems in the principal group's relationship with each of the interacting groups and to develop action plans for solving these problems

Focus

Task
- Performance of the principal group as it interacts with each interdependent group
- Individual group contributions to performance and overall coordination
- Goals and strategies for improving each interacting group's relationship with the principal group

Interpersonal Process
- Intergroup conflict
- Intergroup role conflict
- Intergroup feedback mechanisms
- Intergroup trust
- Intergroup cooperation
- Intergroup climate

Target Group
- At least three interacting work groups (the principal group plus at least two others selected either by the principal group or as a result of needs assessment)

Group Size
- All members or representatives of all groups involved

Setting
- Off site desirable, but on site suitable if the participants can be free from outside disturbances
- Subgroup activities in separate areas if possible

Duration
- Approximately three and one-half to four and one-half days, depending on the number of participants

Methods	• The practitioner and the leaders of all groups involved meet to verify the desire for improved working relationships, to determine goals for the principal group, and to develop a contract.
	• The practitioner meets with all participants to discuss the intervention and its rationale.
	• Data are collected regarding the relationship between the principal group and each of the interacting groups.
	• The members or representatives of all groups meet and receive feedback on the data collected.
	• Through total-group and subgroup work, the participants discuss these data, determine the problems in each interacting group's relationship with the principal group, and develop action plans for solving these problems.
	• The total group reviews the action plans and assigns responsibilities for follow-through.
Rationale for Methods	• The principal group receives constructive feedback on its activities with interacting groups.
	• All involved groups are allowed an opportunity to think through and analyze their working relationships.
	• The emphasis on positive improvement prevents a defensive posture on the part of the principal group.
	• The process allows for constructive reactions and discussion.
	• Intergroup planning takes place.
Probable Content	• One day for the contract session
	• One-half day for the preliminary meeting
	• One day for data collection
	• One to two days for the actual intervention meeting (including subgroup activities)
Practitioner Involvement	• Imperative (either internal or external)
	• Should facilitate review sessions
Time Relevance	• Should follow other activities oriented toward work groups
	• Followed by a session at a later date to review progress

MULTIGROUP MIRROR
ACTION SEQUENCE

1 Contract Session

- Establishing a contract with the leaders of all participating groups
- Setting goals for the principal group

2 Prework Meeting

- Meeting with all participants to describe the objectives and process and to answer related questions

3 Data Collection

- Collecting information from the principal group about its relationship with each interacting group
- Collecting information from each interacting group about its relationship with the principal group

4 Data Feedback

- Posting data collected
- Outlining of data by reporters from the various groups

5 Group Caucuses

- Meeting in original work groups to express reactions to data

6 Group-on-Group Interviews

- Interviewing each interacting group separately about the data while all other participants observe the interview
- Assisting the principal group in discussing learnings thus far while all other participants observe

7 Agenda Development

- Determining important issues to be resolved (in mixed subgroups, each consisting of an interacting group and one or more members of the principal group)
- Sharing issues in the total group
- Rank ordering issues to establish an agenda

8 Mixed-Group Planning

- Developing tentative action plans for dealing with agenda issues (in mixed groups)

9 Joint Action Planning

- Presenting action plans to the total group
- Approving and/or modifying plans
- Assigning responsibilities for follow-through
- Determining deadlines for action
- Establishing a date for a review session

10 Assessment

- Evaluating the experience from a process standpoint
- Making suggestions for the review session

11 Review Session

- Reconvening to review progress and to reaffirm or modify original plans

MULTIGROUP MIRROR
OPERATING PROCEDURE

1. *Contract Session*

   This intervention focuses on a natural work group or a representative cross section of a work-group hierarchy; in addition, other key groups with which this "host" or principal group interacts or representatives of these groups are involved as a "mirror" of the principal group's products or services. The purpose of the intervention is to improve the total work effectiveness of the principal group by concentrating on its interaction with external "clients" or "suppliers" within a total system.* This objective must be incorporated into a contract established with the leaders of all groups that are to participate.

2. *Prework Meeting*

   The practitioner meets with all participants to describe the process to be employed and its rationale. All related questions are answered at this time.

   Depending on several factors, such as the practitioner's preference, the size of the groups involved, and the relationships among the various groups, this step may be combined with step 3.

3. *Data Collection*

   The members of the principal group are interviewed and asked to provide the following information:

   - Their concept of their mission;
   - Adjectives or phrases that describe themselves as they try to carry out this mission;
   - Their concept of each interacting group's mission; and
   - Ways in which they could help each interacting group.

   Then each interacting group is interviewed separately. During each interview the members are asked to provide data on the following subjects:

   - Their concept of their own mission;
   - Their concept of the principal group's mission;
   - Ways in which they could help the principal group; and
   - Ways in which the principal group could help them.

   Each participating group's responses are written on newsprint for posting during step 4.

   The use of this approach avoids putting the principal group in a completely defensive posture when it receives feedback. Defensiveness might result, for example, if

---

*The "Multigroup Mirror" concentrates on the principal group. During the course of this intervention, it may become obvious that the other groups' products or services need specific attention as well; in this case consideration should be given to conducting the intervention entitled "Intergroup Team Building" in this chapter.

at this point the interacting groups were asked to develop long lists of problems originating with the principal group. However, by focusing the groups on opportunities to help each other, an atmosphere conducive to support and constructive change is created for the intervention. In addition, the process of collecting positive information not only generates a data base for the eventual development of solutions to problems; it also reveals a great deal about group roles and purposes, which the authors have found to be the most frequent source of intergroup tension and conflict.

4. *Data Feedback*

The data collected in the previous step are posted in view of all present at the actual intervention meeting. A volunteer from each group in turn is asked to outline his or her group's data, but is cautioned not to defend or elaborate. As each report is made, only questions regarding clarification are entertained. This practice avoids lengthy speeches on the part of reporters and limits them to ensuring a reasonably high level of understanding of the data.

5. *Group Caucuses*

At this point time is allowed for the members of each group to caucus separately to express their reactions to the data presented and to identify issues that they feel are keys to their ongoing interaction with either the principal group or the interacting groups. This forms the basis for the next two steps, but should be held to a maximum of twenty to thirty minutes.

6. *Group-on-Group* Interviews*

The total group is reassembled. Each interacting group in turn meets in the center of a group-on-group configuration; all other participants, including the members of the principal group, serve as the audience. The practitioner questions the group in the center concerning its reactions to the data as discussed during the caucus. A time limit is placed on each group's response period. After all interacting groups have been in the center, the principal group assumes this position and, with the assistance of the practitioner, discusses what it has learned thus far from listening to the various comments.

At this point it is sometimes useful to employ the "open-chair" approach, allowing a member of an interacting group to participate temporarily in the principal group's activity by occupying an empty chair. Prior to this time, however, it is preferable that all "outsiders" simply listen.

7. *Agenda Development*

The participants develop a list of key issues that, if resolved, would increase intergroup effectiveness. This task is accomplished by separating the members of the principal group and assigning one or more of them to each of the interacting groups, which then identifies three or four major agenda items. A time limit of forty-five minutes should be

---

*A group-on-group configuration consists of two groups of participants: One group forms a circle and actively participates in an activity; the other group forms a circle around the first group and observes the first group's activity.

placed on this process, at the end of which the total group reconvenes and shares the individual lists of issues.

8. *Mixed-Group Planning*

One or more principal-group representatives are assigned to meet with each interacting group to develop tentative action plans for dealing with the items that pertain to that particular interacting group. These plans are listed on newsprint for presentation to the joint assembly.

9. *Joint Action Planning*

A spokesperson from each of the groups that completed the previous activity presents his or her group's tentative plans for the approval of and/or modification by all parties involved. Each step of each approved plan is considered separately as an action item, and specific individuals volunteer to take responsibility for follow-through.

The assigning of a deadline for each action item also must be accomplished, but this process should be avoided until all plans have been finalized so that too many commitments are not made for the same time period. After the plans have been developed, usually the participants can quickly establish timetables that avoid conflicts. The practitioner should caution the participants not to set impossible goals for themselves; instead, the amount of time assigned for each task should be liberal to guard against the discouragement afforded by missed deadlines.

After the specifics of all action items have been determined, the practitioner helps the participants to combine the items into a master planning agenda. The final phase of the action-planning process is to set a date for a session to review progress in terms of this agenda.

10. *Assessment*

At the end of the meeting, it is important to ask the participants to assess the entire experience. If bad feelings exist, it is best to surface and confront them while the participants are still together. Encouraging the group to make suggestions for the review session allows the participants to express their feelings about their experience and to determine whether any negativism is shared by others present.

One way to accomplish assessment is to ask the participants to use a rating scale of 1 to 10 to answer questions such as the following:

- How would you rate the quality of our communications? our openness? our plans?
- How optimistic are you regarding follow-through?

11. *Review Session*

After the predetermined period, all parties are reconvened for a half-day review session to rate on a scale of 1 to 10 the quality of their follow-through on the action items. Then those items for which follow-through was rated as low are discussed, either reaffirming the viability of the item and recommitting to its implementation or discarding it as obsolete and considering a better approach.

Before adjourning, another review session should be considered and all participants should be encouraged to continue their efforts. Appropriate compliments should also be given for work to date.

Care should be taken to make this session as positive, constructive, and nonaccusatory as possible, particularly with regard to the treatment of failure to follow through with agreed-on actions. The rationale for this approach is twofold: Unforeseen events may have deterred progress, and the principal group needs to feel supported in its ongoing efforts to improve.

ISSUE CENSUS
OVERVIEW

Objectives
- To examine and improve the effectiveness of a multilevel organizational system or subsystem
- To analyze the entire target system, identifying key issues undermining its effectiveness
- To establish ways to resolve priority issues
- To generate specific goals and action commitments associated with solutions for priority issues

Focus

Task
- The ways in which data are meaningful for the overall organization
- Specific problems implied by the data
- Group performance
- Organizational goals, priorities, long- and short-range strategies, and related goal-setting processes
- Organizational structure, operating procedures, and efficiency
- Specific plans for achieving organizational objectives

Group Maintenance
- Organizational norms
- Subgroups and coalitions
- Role conflict
- Coping capabilities, multilevel and intergroup feedback, cooperation, trust, climate, and conflict

Target Group
- Entire system (or subsystem) if possible; if not, representatives from all organizational levels

Group Size
- Limited only by constraints of time and ability to deal with processing of data
- Thirty to fifty participants, on the average

Setting
- Off site desirable, but on site suitable if the participants can be free from outside disturbances
- Subgroup meetings in separate areas

Duration
- Approximately three days, depending on group size

Methods	• The practitioner and key organizational leaders meet to reach a consensus regarding the objectives, format, and content of the intervention.
	• In subgroups the participants determine organizational strengths, identify negative issues that are operational hindrances, and select the negative issues that are critical to organizational effectiveness.
	• After the subgroups share the results of their work, the total group develops an agenda of negative issues to be addressed and analyzes these issues.
	• The participants form subgroups to brainstorm resolutions for all issues, and these ideas are shared with the total group.
	• An action plan including specific responsibilities and deadlines is developed for resolving each issue.
Rationale for Methods	• The intervention emphasizes candid organizational self-appraisal in a "public" setting with all levels represented.
	• Organizational members can best uncover negative issues and develop effective solutions by sharing perceptions and jointly discussing options.
	• Communication and understanding of organization-wide issues and related action-plan commitment are enhanced among top, middle, and lower organizational levels during joint public discussion.
Probable Content	• One day for the contract session (or as needed depending on the structure of the organization)
	• One-half day of issue generation and sharing
	• One-half day of data consolidation and agenda building
	• One-half day of solution preparation and reporting
	• One-half to one day of action planning, with some time devoted to evaluation of the intervention
Practitioner Involvement	• Imperative that an internal or external practitioner facilitate the intervention
Time Relevance	• Often useful as a first step in analyzing total organizational effectiveness, instituting organization-wide change, and quickly improving communication and commitment
	• Provides an excellent follow-up to other interventions or an alternative to annual employee meetings or management conferences
	• Followed by a session at a later date to review progress

ISSUE CENSUS
ACTION SEQUENCE

1

Initial Contract Session(s)

- Discussing the following with organizational leaders: felt needs; mutual expectations; overall strategy, format, and content; and related logistics

2

Data Collection and Issue Identification

- Dividing into subgroups to determine organizational strengths and weaknesses
- Screening data in subgroups to select major issues that require work

3

Data Feedback

- Summarizing the results of the work

4

Agenda Building

- Reviewing overall data and developing an agenda of priority issues requiring resolution

5

Data Analysis

- Sharing feelings about the agenda items
- Analyzing each item in detail

6

Option Generation

- Brainstorming issue resolutions in subgroups

7

Action Planning

- Sharing brainstormed ideas
- Modifying suggestions until consensus is reached on all solutions
- Developing plans of action to ensure implementation of solutions
- Setting a date for a review session

8

Assessment

- Evaluating the session from the standpoint of both content and process

9

Review Session

- Reconvening to evaluate progress to date
- Developing further plans to ensure continued implementation

ISSUE CENSUS
OPERATING PROCEDURE

1. *Initial Contract Session(s)*

This phase typically takes place two to four weeks prior to the actual intervention meeting. Its primary purpose is to obtain agreement from the key organizational leaders whose subordinates will participate as to objectives, potential benefits, format, and content. Because this intervention is aimed at an entire organization (or at least a major subsystem) and thus involves multiple levels of management, it is often necessary to hold several contract sessions in sequence, beginning with top-level leadership and proceeding downward. The practitioner confirms the felt needs for which the intervention is designed and discusses mutual expectations. The relationship between the practitioner and the organizational leadership should be clearly outlined, and related questions and concerns should be dealt with. Management's concept of potential problems also should be elicited.

In addition, the leaders should be encouraged to be very supportive of openness and candor on the part of subordinates, both prior to and during the intervention meeting; such support helps to overcome the concern of participants at all levels that valid data may not be obtained because of the inhibiting presence of top leadership. One option available to the practitioner and useful in some large target systems is to arrange for top executives and/or administrators to participate only in the later phases of the intervention meeting. This approach not only enhances the energy-releasing power of openness on the part of those likely to be inhibited by the early presence of top management; it also capitalizes on the reinforcing power of top management's approval of actions already planned.

Another matter that must be dealt with during contracting is the way in which subgroups will be organized for the meeting. The prime consideration is enhancement of the generation of valid data. In general, subgroups of four to eight participants each allow for ample individual participation. Care should be taken to avoid placing supervisors and subordinates in the same subgroup. Stratification horizontally often makes sense, as does grouping by either function or territory. In any case the method to be used should be established and approved at this time.

2. *Data Collection and Issue Identification*

This phase opens the intervention meeting and should be preceded by an appropriate introduction. To plunge into data generation without stimulating openness is usually counterproductive. The introduction need not be lengthy, but it should clarify expectations and culminate in the participants' acceptance of related norms for the meeting.

After establishing norms the practitioner explains that the process of data collection is to be accomplished in subgroups. Care should be taken at this point to ensure that all participants clearly understand the data-collection task. This task is to list the major strengths of the organization that contribute positively to success and the key issues that constitute hindrances to success; from the list of negative issues identified, the members of each subgroup are to select three or four that they are most interested in dealing with during the course of the intervention. In addition, each subgroup is to choose a reporter, whose responsibility is to summarize the subgroup's decisions and to present this summary to the total group.

When the task has been clarified, subgroups are organized according to the method decided during contracting. Materials such as tape, newsprint flip charts, and felt-tipped markers are distributed, and each subgroup is assigned a meeting place and a deadline for task completion. Then the subgroups are dismissed to work on their assignments.

It is useful for the practitioner to check with each subgroup at least once or twice during the first thirty minutes to ensure that the members understand the assignment, are organized, and are not bogged down in discussion of a given item. In the early stages they usually need to be reminded to defer discussion until they have listed as many items as possible. When the participants are having difficulty reaching a consensus regarding items to be listed, it helps to stipulate that although at least two individuals should agree on the validity of each listed item, unanimity is not required.

After both positive and negative issues have been listed, each subgroup establishes the priority of the negative issues, separating the major concerns from relatively minor ones and focusing on matters that are critical to organizational effectiveness.

3. *Data Feedback*

The total group is reconvened. The subgroup reporters summarize the data generated, answering questions regarding clarification only. The practitioner should ensure that discussion at this stage is limited to developing an understanding of the issues; reactions, responses, and debate should be discouraged. Otherwise, the participants may waste time discussing negative issues that are determined to be low-priority items. Each reporter should be encouraged to be brief and to respond to requests for clarification in any way that he or she finds comfortable.

4. *Agenda Building*

At this point the practitioner assists the group in developing a consolidated agenda of negative issues for in-depth discussion. Almost inevitably some of the subgroup issues overlap; these items need to be combined, transferred to a master agenda, listed in order of priority, and reduced to a manageable number. The practitioner should caution the participants not to list a larger number of issues than they can reasonably handle in the time available for the intervention; if some participants object to the elimination of certain items, the practitioner should reassure them by suggesting that a record of lower-priority issues be kept for future reference and attention. However, this does not mean that the practitioner should avoid confronting some subgroups regarding their tendencies to bypass or minimize the importance of issues that are potentially controversial, such as matters of interpersonal conflict and dysfunctional behavior. On the contrary, the authors feel that the practitioner owes it to the client to confront such evasions of responsibility and should not hesitate to share with the group the consequences that may result from refusing to deal with controversial issues. Indeed, the presence of the practitioner may make this occasion the ideal time to tackle the more-difficult issues since many of the "safer" ones can often be handled later without the help of a practitioner. In addition, the group may not be capable of dealing with simpler issues until the more-difficult ones have been resolved.

Thus, the practitioner should respond to the participants' discomfort by helping them to confront their anxieties about perceived risks. Obviously, certain trade-offs are involved because the group needs to own its norms about risk taking. Ultimately, the practitioner must establish a balance between the obligation to respect client rights to remain silent and the obligation to encourage candid confrontation so that the intervention is successful.

5. *Data Analysis*

This phase allows the participants an opportunity to share their feelings about the agreed-on agenda items. Without this period of catharsis, the authors have found that few groups can move beyond disagreements to joint ownership of plans and solutions.

The process of sharing can be facilitated in several ways. One way is to assign a time frame for each agenda and to encourage any and all responses to such questions as the following:

- What is the source of the problem?
- What is the essence of the problem?
- Are we addressing cause or effect?
- What are the effects of the problem on employee behavior and performance?

By observing nonverbal behavior and intervening primarily to encourage responses, the practitioner can usually help the group to progress through the entire agenda in a few hours.

An optional approach is to deal with each item in its entirety before moving to the next item; after sufficient time has been devoted to open discussion of an issue, the group proceeds to the next phase by proposing options for resolution (see step 6). This approach offers the advantage of generating solutions while the issue is still fresh on everyone's mind; in addition, it provides the group with a sense of progress.

Yet another option is to assign specific agenda items to subgroups for analysis, asking for reports within a given time frame. This option is particularly useful with large groups to ensure that everyone has a chance to contribute.

6. *Option Generation*

For this step the participants are assembled into subgroups, each of which is asked to capitalize on the previous discussion by brainstorming and listing on newsprint possible solutions or vehicles for improvement for all issues. Each subgroup should be encouraged to list as many options as possible for each issue; no single recommendation should occupy the subgroup's attention at this point.

7. *Action Planning*

Preliminary solutions and ideas from step 6 are shared with the total group. All participants are invited to respond to these presentations and to modify suggestions as necessary until a consensus is reached regarding the appropriate way to deal with each issue. Then the group develops a step-by-step plan of action to ensure implementation of each solution. This process may be approached in one of two ways. The first is to focus the entire group on developing a sequential plan for the resolution of each issue that includes answers to the following questions:

- What specific tasks must be performed?
- Who is to be responsible for performing these tasks?
- How and in what sequence are the tasks to be completed?
- What deadlines should be established?

Another approach can be selected when subgroups have been employed in the preceding step. For each solution that the group decides to adopt, the subgroup that originated that solution is asked to draft a plan of action for approval and/or modification by the total group.

The authors have found that the time consumed by these two options is about the same. The time saved by not forming subgroups is offset by the time required to allow everyone to voice opinions. Conversely, the time saved by having subgroups work simultaneously on developing action plans is offset by the time required to report the subgroup results and then achieve total-group consensus.

The last part of this step consists of setting a date for a session to review progress. Also, the practitioner should explain that he or she plans to maintain a record of the various deadlines established and to contact key leaders periodically before the review session to offer assistance and to inquire about progress.*

8. *Assessment*

It is important that the participants evaluate their ability to work together in a session of this nature and consider related process issues. It is also important that the participants leave the session with a clear perception of the way in which the entire group rated the experience. Accordingly, the practitioner should ask the group to rate several key dimensions on a scale of 1 to 10. Questions such as the following should be asked:

- Were the right issues dealt with?
- Were we open and candid?
- How would you rate the quality of the action plans?
- What is your level of optimism regarding follow-through?
- How beneficial was the overall session?

9. *Review Session*

During this step the entire group reconvenes to assess progress to date in light of the original deadlines; to reaffirm the viability of the action plans; to discuss unforeseen developments that may have occurred and to make necessary adjustments in response to these developments; and to make further plans to ensure follow-through, including another review session. The authors recommend that the practitioner facilitate this session to help ensure openness, participation, and proper examination of follow-through.

---

*These periodic checks are often critical to offset the inertia that frequently occurs when the participants leave the intervention setting. In the authors' opinion, one of the key mistakes made by inexperienced OD practitioners is assuming that such inquiries are inappropriate or unnecessary.

INTERGROUP TEAM BUILDING
OVERVIEW

Objectives
- To examine and improve the total work effectiveness of two interdependent work groups
- To provide an opportunity for the two groups to disclose perceptions of each other in terms of positive or negative (helpful/harmful) contributions to one another's work effectiveness, impact on overall effectiveness, individual and mutual goals, and specific actions that occur in each area
- To identify problem areas and corrective actions for each group and for joint remedies

Focus

Task
- Group performance (considered separately and together)
- Individual group contributions to performance and overall coordination
- Group goals, long- and short-range strategies, and goal-setting processes
- Specific plans for individuals in connection with group and intergroup roles
- Intergroup make-up and structure, operating procedures, and efficiency

Interpersonal Process
- Group norms/cultures
- Group identity
- Group and intergroup role conflict
- Individual and group conflict
- Mutuality of goals
- Superordinate goals
- Intergroup feedback process
- Intergroup conflict resolution
- Intergroup trust
- Intergroup cooperation

Target Group
- Two interacting work groups

Group Size
- All members of both groups

Setting
- Off site desirable, but on site suitable if the participants can be free from outside disturbances

Duration
- Approximately three and one-half days, depending on group size and objectives

Methods	• The practitioner and the group leaders meet to verify the desire for improved working relationships and to determine commitment to follow through on recommendations. • A preliminary meeting is held with each group separately to outline the objectives, format, and content of the intervention and to answer questions. • In separate meetings the groups generate lists that detail their perceptions of each other. • All participants meet to receive feedback on the data collected. • The two groups caucus separately to express reactions to the data; then each group in turn discusses its reactions while the other group observes. • The participants identify key issues to be resolved, form subgroups to determine plans for resolutions, and present these plans to the total group. • The resolution plans are modified and accepted, and deadlines and responsibilities for follow-through are determined.
Rationale for Methods	• The groups engage in a candid appraisal of their own interactions. • Teamwork is enhanced when group members become better acquainted, especially in terms of work-style preferences and particular work conditions and pressures. • The groups are given an opportunity to think through and analyze their working relationships. • Because the emphasis is on problem resolution, defensiveness is minimized. • Intergroup planning takes place.
Probable Content	• One day for the contracting session • One-half day for the prework meeting • Two days for the actual intervention meeting (with approximately half of the time spent in original groups)
Practitioner Involvement	• Imperative as internal or external facilitator
Time Relevance	• Usually follows other activities oriented toward natural work groups • Followed by a session at a later date to review progress

INTERGROUP TEAM BUILDING
ACTION SEQUENCE

1
Contract Session

- Discussing needs, expectations, and the details of the project with the group leaders

2
Prework Meetings

- Meeting with each group separately to outline the process and objectives and to answer questions

3
Data Collection

- Meeting with each group separately to collect data on perceptions of each other and intergroup relations
- Selecting representatives from each group to present their own group's data during the feedback session

4
Data Feedback

- Presenting results of data collection and clarifying as necessary

5
Team Caucuses

- Meeting briefly in original work groups to share reactions to the data

6
Group-on-Group Discussions

- Assisting each group in turn with data discussion while the other group observes

7
Agenda Building

- Identifying key issues to be resolved

8
Mixed-Group Planning

- Forming mixed groups to work on designated issues
- Developing preliminary proposals for resolution

9
Joint Action Planning

- Presenting proposals for resolution to the entire group
- Modifying and accepting the proposals
- Assigning responsibilities for follow-through
- Determining deadlines for action
- Establishing a date for a review session

10
Assessment

- Evaluating the experience in terms of content and process

11
Review Session

- Meeting as planned to examine progress to date and to reaffirm or modify original plans

INTERGROUP TEAM BUILDING
OPERATING PROCEDURE

1. *Contract Session*

This session typically takes place several weeks prior to the actual intergroup event and focuses on ensuring that the work-group leaders are comfortable with the process that will take place. During this meeting the practitioner clarifies the process as well as the potential payoffs for both groups. This clarification helps to ensure a degree of consistency in the leaders' explanations to their respective subordinates; it also helps to promote the leaders' commitment to the success of the project.

The sequence of events, the rationale for various activities, role expectations, and related timing and logistics need to be established at this time. The authors have also found it helpful to spend some time encouraging the leaders to act as naturally and spontaneously as possible during the intervention so that an open atmosphere prevails.

2. *Prework Meetings*

It is highly recommended that a preliminary meeting be held with each group separately to outline the objectives, format, and content of the process and to answer questions. If the practitioner wishes, these meetings can be handled in conjunction with step 3. The purpose of the meetings is to minimize the rumors and fantasies often associated with an intergroup session. Participants frequently assume that such an intervention will be fraught with conflict that may worsen relations between the two groups. In the authors' experience a significant number of participants who are involved in their first intergroup team-building session begin the experience with varying degrees of skepticism about the need for such a session or its potential for success. This is particularly true of groups whose past interactions have been riddled with various forms of conflict. In these cases participants have often been required to attend numerous meetings over a period of years to try to resolve issues that they predict will be raised again and again. Thus, they approach yet another attempt at resolution with something less than optimism, and they need to be exposed to a process involving factors and methods that are different from those that have typified past meetings.

To begin such a meeting, the group leader provides an appropriate introduction and an expression of support for the objectives of the session. Then the practitioner explains the action sequence in detail, answering questions from the group as candidly as possible.

One approach to ensuring that the objectives of the meeting are achieved is to obtain anonymous questions or concerns in writing from the group members at the outset of the presentation. These data are then used to guide the focus of the discussion.

3. *Data Collection*

In separate meetings the members of each group generate lists that include the following data:

- A statement of their own mission. The members write one or two sentences explaining the purpose for which their group exists in terms of the service or product that it provides and for whom.

- A statement of the other group's mission. The members define the perceived purpose for which the other group exists.

- Adjectives or phrases that describe their own performance and behavior as they attempt to carry out their mission. (At this point the members should be encouraged not to let modesty inhibit their self-descriptions.)

- Adjectives or phrases that describe the performance and behavior of the members of the other group in attempting to carry out their mission. This list is generated for the use of the other group. (Again, candor should be encouraged. It is a good idea to stipulate that although no item will be listed without the support of at least two group members, no item requires unanimity. Making this stipulation and assuring the participants that the members of the other group will be apprised of the stipulation can often overcome hesitance to share perceptions.)

- Predictions about the way in which they are viewed by the members of the other group. (Whether these predictions prove accurate or not, they are almost always educational.)

- Ways in which they could help the other group. The members list things that they could do, stop doing, or do more or less frequently to assist the other group in accomplishing its mission. (Because this activity requires at least some willingness to consider changes that might be helpful, it is particularly useful for defusing any hostility that might have developed as a result of generating other data.)

- Ways in which the other group could help them. This activity provides an opportunity to identify or reaffirm specific actions on the part of the other group that would improve intergroup effectiveness. These ideas usually identify the basis of intergroup problems and provide the keys to agenda building. (It is important to encourage the group members to be as specific as possible without exhausting them or forcing them to lose sight of major items while concentrating on those of relatively little importance.)

Other types of information may be obtained as well. Although some practitioners who conduct such team-building sessions prefer to have each group generate a list of complaints about the other group, the authors have found that emphasizing positive factors avoids unnecessary or counterproductive negativism and still allows major issues to surface.

It is possible to collect data on the morning of the first intervention day if necessary to condense the project into as short a time frame as feasible. However, it is preferable to have the groups generate these lists a few days prior to the actual session. Not only does this approach allow the groups an opportunity to rest after expending the energy necessary to generate data; it also allows both groups to spend time thinking about the data instead of dealing with them immediately in an intergroup setting.

During this step representatives from each group are selected to explain their own group's data to the members of the other group when feedback takes place.

4. *Data Feedback*

In a meeting attended by all participants, the representatives selected in the previous step present the data. Each data subject is dealt with separately, with the representatives contributing all relevant information. At this time only questions regarding clarification are accepted. The practitioner may assist by gently but firmly enforcing this rule so that premature analyses are not undertaken before each group understands the other's data.

Each reporter should be instructed to avoid filibustering and to respond to requests for clarification in any way with which he or she feels comfortable. The remaining members of each group should be encouraged to help their representatives to answer questions. In addition, all participants should be reminded that few if any specific items were unanimous. (This reminder relieves the discomfort of those participants who disagree with certain perceptions held by their own groups.)

5. *Team Caucuses*

At this point it is useful to release tension by asking each group to caucus separately to express reactions to the data. Group members are generally more open and participative during the next step if they have at least a general sense of their colleagues' opinions with respect to some of the key points of the other group's data. When giving instructions for caucusing, the practitioner should encourage the members of each group to share their reactions to and feelings about the data, their learnings thus far as a result of listening to the reports, and possibilities for clearing up misunderstandings. Having both groups caucus in the same room not only saves time but also helps to guard against the feelings of polarization that often develop as a result of physical separation.

6. *Group-on-Group* Discussions*

The total group is reconvened. Each original group in turn meets in the center of a group-on-group configuration to discuss reactions to the data while the remaining group observes. The usual rule about silence on the part of those in the outer circle is enforced; however, an "open" chair in the inner circle is provided so that anyone from the outer group who wishes to participate may occupy this chair and do so. During these discussions the practitioner takes notes on various possibilities for identification as major issues.

One valuable aspect of this step is the opportunity for catharsis. Without this opportunity tension might block effective interaction during the rest of the intervention.

7. *Agenda Building*

At this point the two groups work to identify a manageable number of key issues to be resolved. One approach to this step is to have the two groups caucus again to determine major agenda items. However, to save time the practitioner can simply list a number of possibilities and ask the participants to modify this list as they wish.

Regardless of the approach taken, it is important to limit the items to those over which the two groups have sufficient control to develop viable resolutions. It is also important to restrict choices to high-priority items so that all can be dealt with during the session. The latter restriction is particularly critical if part of the first day has been devoted to data collection. Participants often tend to be overly ambitious with regard to the number of items to be addressed; if this is the case, the practitioner should suggest that future meetings be scheduled to deal with low-priority issues.

---

*A group-on-group configuration consists of two groups of participants: One group forms a circle and actively participates in an activity; the other group forms a circle around the first group and observes the first group's activity.

8. *Mixed-Group Planning*

For each major issue identified, representatives from both groups are asked to develop a written plan for resolution. To select representatives the two groups can be asked to caucus separately to make decisions based on their own criteria, or the practitioner can simply call for volunteers. In either case the practitioner should emphasize the necessity for organizing quickly to start planning.

After the selections have been made, the practitioner should ensure that everyone clearly understands his or her assignment. The actual work assigned to each group of representatives depends on the complexity of the issue. The group may be asked to determine a direct solution for presentation to the entire assembly at the end of the planning phase, or it may be instructed to develop a multiple-step plan for reaching solution within a specific time. If the latter course is indicated, the practitioner should recommend that the group also establish specific task assignments and appropriate deadlines. Equipped with felt-tipped markers and newsprint flip charts, the mixed groups then retire to a designated area for negotiation and planning.

When the data have been collected prior to the intervention meeting, the participants are usually ready for this step by early afternoon of the first day. In this case they can spend the rest of the day completing their assignments and preparing reports for presentation the next morning.

9. *Joint Action Planning*

Representatives from each mixed group post the results of their work, deliver a presentation to the entire assembly, answer questions, and begin to obtain total-group support. Often the practitioner's only responsibility at this point will be to elicit suggestions for modifying each plan as proposed, ensuring that a clear, written commitment to specific, time-delimited action is obtained. However, the authors' experience indicates that the practitioner may need to assume a more directive role during this step than adopted previously, especially with participants who have had no experience with this type of process. Some plans may require major changes, and usually the process of making these changes is expedited when the practitioner takes charge. This is not always the case, of course, and the practitioner must be sensitive to maintaining the crucial balance between ownership and the time available. Ultimately this process should yield a written document for each issue that delineates resolution in terms of responsibilities and deadlines.

In addition, a date should be set for a session to review progress, renew commitments, and modify plans as necessary. This session should be scheduled far enough in the future to allow both groups time to gain experience in following through with negotiated agreements, but soon enough to correct any plans that start going awry. Time spans vary, but are typically three to nine months in length.

10. *Assessment*

Although the participants are often anxious to leave after dealing with all issues and setting a review date, it is important that the meeting not be adjourned until the group has processed the experience. This practice clarifies the participants' level of commitment to their action plans and reveals any misperceptions about the meeting.

It is helpful to ask the participants to evaluate the experience by rating certain aspects on a scale of 1 to 10. The following questions may be asked:

- Were the right issues surfaced?
- Were we open and honest?
- How would you rate the quality of the action plans?
- What is your level of optimism regarding follow-through?
- Was the practitioner helpful?
- How would you rate the overall meeting?

This assessment should be made a part of the information that is distributed to all participants.

11. *Review Session*

During this session the practitioner facilitates a review of each original action item. It is helpful for the original groups to caucus separately to rate progress on each item on a scale of 1 to 10, using appropriate criteria such as "overall follow-through to date" and so forth. These evaluations are then shared in the total group, and the participants process their rationales for the ratings and their feelings about their progress.

Appropriate modifications or additional plans are then developed to accommodate interim experience and to ensure ongoing commitment. The practitioner leads the group away from recriminations or accusations regarding follow-through failure, encouraging a focus on reaffirming the viability of the plans and the payoffs to all concerned.

ORGANIZATIONAL STRUCTURE

The interventions in Chapter 5 were designed to meet diagnosed needs that frequently arise during the typical life cycles of natural work groups. The primary targets common to those interventions were the sociosystem and process-system components of an organization as defined in Chapter 2; in other words, the focus was primarily the behavioral aspect of strategic change techniques. In contrast, the interventions presented in this chapter concentrate on *technosystem* components, which include organizational goals, priorities, task, and mission; hierarchical structure, job design, and reward and support systems; and related structures of policies, practices, and procedures.

As stated in Chapter 2, examination of organizational issues and opportunities starts with the social system (the behavioral aspect), proceeds to the related key processes (decision making, problem solving, communication, and so forth), and finally arrives at the structures that constitute the technosystem. Many managers feel that it is more natural to attack organizational problems in this order, either because they are more likely to notice sociosystem and process-system problems first because of the associated pain and frustration or because they perceive sociosystem and process-system solutions as less risky than those aimed at structural change. To many executives, administrators, and managers, the risks associated with engaging in one of the team-building interventions, for example, appear more acceptable than those associated with interventions that produce change in the hierarchical structure or the content of jobs or policy. In addition, organizational leaders who do endeavor to alter the technosystem are often preoccupied during such an intervention with the more immediate tactical problems that are facing them in the next few weeks; consequently, they have difficulty in concentrating on long-term strategic planning.

Nevertheless, to conduct joint problem analysis that not only is systematically planned and reflective of humanistic values but also produces valid data and then to fail to deal with technosystem issues is to negate the efforts involved in the interventions of Chapter 5. Often, in the process of using the sociosystem and process-system interventions, structural issues are revealed and demand appropriate action.

INTERVENTION CATEGORIES

The designs in this chapter are organized as follows.

1. An intervention that is associated with clarifying a given work unit's mission, goals, and priorities for a specified period and that takes advantage of management-by-objectives (MBO) payoffs on a group and organization-wide basis:

   • Team Goal Setting

2. Interventions that are associated with obtaining information about an entire organizational structure, including its mission, strengths, and weaknesses; developing related strategic plans at the top; and involving all employees in working to resolve those issues that are best treated at the level of the natural work group:

   - Strategic Planning
   - Survey-Guided Development

3. An intervention that is aimed at effective development of a totally new organizational structure:

   - New-Plant Start-Up

4. Interventions that deal with the definition and development of the job content that is most likely to utilize and motivate human resources effectively, to clarify role expectations, and to resolve related conflict:

   - Job Development
   - Role Development

TEAM GOAL SETTING
OVERVIEW

Objectives
- To generate goals and a related action plan to which a work group is committed as a team
- To clarify the team's mission and related accountabilities, minimizing role confusion and focusing group energy
- To take advantage of MBO benefits at the group level, ensuring a high level of group interaction and cohesiveness

Focus

Task
- Team goals, tasks, methods, and priorities
- Team mission, structure, accountabilities, and operating procedure
- Specific plans for team goal accomplishment, including individual assignments
- Analytical examination of related facts, assumptions, and potential problems associated with team objectives

Group Maintenance
- Team identity, norms, and culture
- Individual-/group-conflict management
- Mutuality of goals and accountabilities
- Superordinate goals
- Team/individual allegiance and focus
- Problem ownership
- Role conflict
- Interpersonal cooperation

Target Group
- A natural work group (supervisor and subordinates)

Group Size
- All members of the target group

Setting
- Off site preferable, but on site suitable if the participants can be free from outside disturbances

Duration
- Approximately two days, depending on the size of the group and the complexity of the planning

Methods
- The team composes a mission statement defining the purpose of its existence.
- Related accountabilities are determined.
- Goals associated with team accountabilities are identified.
- The team identifies the intergroup coordination and/or cooperation required to accomplish each goal.
- The participants determine facts, assumptions, and potential problems associated with each goal.
- An action plan is developed for each goal.

Rationale for Methods

- Teams require clear goals to ensure focused energy, ownership, and commitment.
- To avoid dysfunctional competition and to ensure cooperation, individuals require a high level of understanding of the team mission and the ways in which individual responsibilities support team accountabilities.
- Individual ownership of and commitment to team goals evolve from participation in their development.
- Examination of interrelationships between individuals and interfacing groups is necessary to ensure a high level of optimistic commitment.

Practitioner Involvement

- Ensures proper focus during process as well as comprehensiveness of goals established

Time Relevance

- Excellent initiating event for an improvement effort, but can be initiated at almost any point during a work group's life

TEAM GOAL SETTING
ACTION SEQUENCE

1

Development of a Team-Mission Statement

- Composing a statement regarding the team's purpose, "customers," and unique attributes

2

Development of Team Accountabilities

- Determining results and/or conditions for which the team will be accountable

3

Identification of Lower-Level Accountabilities

- Identifying accountabilities that should be delegated to lower-level teams
- Determining parameters for each lower-level item
- Establishing a method for communicating these items to lower-level teams

4

Goal Brainstorming

- Generating possible goals associated with accountabilities, lower-level feedback, and related team concerns

5

Development of Team-Goal Criteria

- Developing criteria for identifying final team goals

6

Goal Identification

- Employing criteria to screen goals brainstormed in step 4

7

Determination of Cooperative Goals

- Deciding which goals require working with other teams

8

Goal-Information Brainstorming

- Generating information pertinent to achieving each goal

9

Action Planning

- Establishing a plan of action for achieving each goal

TEAM GOAL SETTING
OPERATING PROCEDURE

1. *Development of a Team-Mission Statement*

   The team-mission statement should incorporate answers to the following questions:
   - What is the team's specific purpose or reason for being?
   - Whom (or which groups) does the team serve?
   - What are the team's unique qualities as a unit?

   To develop such a statement, the team members work individually for a few minutes to answer these questions and then share the results of their work with the total group. After sharing, the members consolidate their individual ideas into a group statement. The practitioner may find that larger groups can be handled more effectively by forming subgroups and asking each to draft a statement; this process is followed by total-group sharing and consolidating.

2. *Development of Team Accountabilities*

   A team's "accountabilities" are the specific results and/or conditions for which it expects to be held uniquely answerable after a given time period. Such results or conditions should be exclusive to the particular team involved and consistent with the mission statement developed in the previous step; in addition, they should reflect outcomes rather than activities.

   Each team member should be asked to work individually to list his or her own accountabilities. Then the participants are polled, and the individual determinations are listed and displayed for the entire group. At this point criteria are established for translating *individual* accountabilities into *team* accountabilities; for example, a team accountability might be one that applies to two or more members. All individual accountabilities listed previously are screened according to the agreed-on criteria. Those that are determined to be team accountabilities are then divided into logical clusters of items that are similar to or extensions of each other.

3. *Identification of Lower-Level Accountabilities*

   Some accountabilities that are not assigned to the team list may, nevertheless, support the team's accountabilities and make real and direct contributions to the organizational level of which the team is a part. Such accountabilities may represent items for delegation to lower-level teams consisting of the participants' subordinates. If the participants decide that this is the case, for each lower-level accountability they should develop and agree on specific parameters, determine appropriate wording, and establish a method for communicating the accountability to the appropriate lower-level team. After completing this step the group is adjourned for the day so that the participants can discuss these accountability items with their subordinates and obtain feedback.

4. *Goal Brainstorming*

   This step begins the second day of the intervention meeting. The group brainstorms goals associated with the accomplishment of each team accountability, feedback from subordinates, perceived changes needed, and performance maintenance. If the group is particularly large, this task can be accomplished in subgroups, which subsequently share their ideas with the total group.

5. *Development of Team-Goal Criteria*

The participants develop criteria that they feel should be used in identifying final team goals. Examples of such criteria include the following:

- practicality
- team control over accomplishment
- probability of achievement
- measurability

6. *Goal Identification*

The list of goals developed in step 4 is screened against the criteria established in step 5, thus identifying goals to which the team feels it can commit itself.

7. *Determination of Cooperative Goals*

The participants determine which goals require cooperation and/or coordination with other work teams.

8. *Goal-Information Brainstorming*

For each goal identified, the participants brainstorm the following information:

- facts presently known
- assumptions and predictions
- potential problems associated with its accomplishment

9. *Action Planning*

The team engages in development of an action plan for each goal, incorporating answers to the following questions:

- What objectives must be accomplished?
- How will they be accomplished?
- How will progress be measured?
- Who will be responsible for accomplishing the objectives?
- What will the related time frames be?

STRATEGIC PLANNING
OVERVIEW

Objectives
- To identify strengths and weaknesses, both current and future, in relation to mission accomplishment in the organization
- To identify environmental factors that presently influence the organization's effectiveness, forecasting their future impact
- To generate specific strategies, plans, goals, and objectives to which the organization is committed to ensure that the problems identified are resolved

Focus

Task

- Group awareness of future issues and factors likely to affect performance
- Group goals, long- and short-range strategies, and goal-setting processes
- Specific plans and objectives for individuals as they relate to group action plans
- Development of contingency plans and solutions to forecasted problems

Group Maintenance
- Group identity, individual allegiance, and focus
- Capabilities for coping
- Mutuality of goals
- Superordinate goals
- Problem ownership
- Assumption testing

Target Group
- The organization's management

Group Size
- All members of the organization's management if possible; if not, representatives from all levels of management

Setting
- Off site preferable, but on site suitable if the participants can be free from outside disturbances

Methods
- The participants define the organizational mission in two or three sentences.
- The group brainstorms current strengths and weaknesses associated with the accomplishment of the organizational mission.
- Major restraints and environmental arenas within which the organization operates are identified.
- For each of these restraints or arenas, the group determines facts as well as assumptions about the future.
- The group identifies specific organizational goals and objectives required to accommodate or to react to the organizational mission, strengths and weaknesses, and the facts and assumptions about operational restraints and environmental arenas.
- The goals and objectives are translated into specific, time-delimited action plans that include accountability considerations.

Rationale for Methods	• Effective medium- and long-range strategies can be developed with the maximum involvement of those who are expected to commit themselves to their implementation.
	• In order to discuss strategic plans, those involved must clearly understand and accept the organization's mission.
	• To minimize time-wasting digression during planning, it is essential to separate facts from assumptions.
	• If managers are to develop appropriate change plans, they must examine the interrelationships among the operational restraints and environmental arenas affecting their organization.
Practitioner Involvement	• Highly recommended as the facilitator of the intervention meeting
	• Not essential for review session
Time Relevance	• Excellent initiating event for organizational-improvement effort
	• Good response to an identified need for improved planning
	• Followed by a session at a later date to review progress

STRATEGIC PLANNING
ACTION SEQUENCE

1

Development of an Organizational-Mission Statement

- Defining the organizational mission in two or three sentences

2

Identification of Strengths and Weaknesses

- Listing assets and liabilities that affect mission accomplishment

3

Assessment of Operational Restraints and Environmental Arenas

- Listing key restraints and arenas within which the organization must operate

4

Determination of Facts and Assumptions

- Listing facts as well as assumptions about the future for each key restraint and environmental arena

5

Goal Identification

- Identifying goals related to the organization's mission, strengths and weaknesses, and current and future assessments of key restraints and arenas

6

Generation of Objectives

- Determining individual objectives for the more complex goals identified in step 5

7

Action Planning

- Writing a plan of action for achieving each goal and each objective of more complex goals
- Establishing a date for the review session

8

Review Session

- Reviewing progress toward achieving each goal
- Developing further action plans or modifying original ones as necessary

STRATEGIC PLANNING
OPERATING PROCEDURE

1. *Development of an Organizational-Mission Statement*

   In this phase the management group develops a two- to three-sentence summary statement defining the mission and purpose of the organization. This statement not only provides a basis for the steps that follow but also serves as a reference point.

2. *Identification of Strengths and Weaknesses*

   The practitioner assists the management group in listing current strengths and weaknesses that are perceived as being associated with the accomplishment of the organization's mission. The listed items are intended to reflect overall assets and liabilities with regard to resources, constraints, and impact on mission accomplishment.

3. *Assessment of Operational Restraints and Environmental Arenas*

   Using the data generated in step 2 as stimuli, the practitioner helps the group to brainstorm a list of restraints and environmental arenas within which the organization must operate and to which the organization must remain sensitive if it is to succeed in its mission. This list is then pared down to a manageable number of key restraints and arenas (usually six to eight) for which appropriate plans need to be made to ensure viability in the foreseeable future. Examples include markets, financing, employee population, community relations, local economy, and competition.

4. *Determination of Facts and Assumptions*

   The group separately analyzes each of the key restraints and arenas, first listing the facts that can be supported with empirical data and that represent the *present* condition insofar as it is known by the participants. Then the group lists a set of assumptions or educated guesses about the *future* condition of each restraint and arena.

5. *Goal Identification*

   The practitioner helps the participants to identify several goals that seem related to the mission of the organization, its strengths and weaknesses, and the group's current and future assessments of key restraints and arenas. These goals should be limited to a manageable number of high-priority targets stated in terms specific enough to be translated into action plans for achieving the objectives to be developed in the next step.

6. *Generation of Objectives*

   Although some of the goals identified in the previous step may be of a type that is simple enough to warrant one direct plan of action, others may be more complex and require that several smaller objectives be met before the goals themselves can be achieved. This phase of the intervention consists of setting such objectives as necessary.

7. *Action Planning*

   With the help of the practitioner, the participants write a plan of action for achieving each goal. To help ensure follow-through and success, each plan is developed in a detailed fashion, concentrating on the accomplishment of each objective where applicable. A typical plan details how each objective will be met, who will coordinate and be primarily responsible for follow-up and with whom he or she will work, and when the objective will be reached (in terms of specifically identified milestones in pursuit of its accomplishment).

Depending on the time available for this phase, assignments may need to be made for developing plans of action to be considered by the group in a separate session. However, in this stage the group should at least develop skeletal outlines that are specific enough to guide further work. In addition, arrangements should be made for copies of all action plans as well as useful backup data from steps 1 through 6 to be distributed to all members of the group.

Before adjournment the group also determines a date for reconvening to review progress on each action plan. This date should not be so far in the future as to preclude mid-course correction as required by unforeseen circumstances; however, it should not be so soon that the time allowed for follow-through is insufficient.

8. *Review Session*

The agenda for this session is a detailed review of progress toward achieving each goal. In addition, the group works on developing further plans or modifying the original ones as dictated by experience and circumstance.

SURVEY-GUIDED DEVELOPMENT
OVERVIEW

Objectives
- To take a measurement of an entire organization
- To improve organizational effectiveness by surveying all employees, feeding back resulting data through individual work groups, and developing analyses and problem-resolution plans in response to these data

Focus

Task

- The ways in which data are meaningful for individual work groups and the total organization
- Specific problems implied by the data
- Patterns in the data that reveal particular concerns or strengths
- Development of solutions and specific, corrective actions to be taken
- Development of requests for explanations needed from other levels or other groups in the organization
- Determination of problems that require assistance from other levels or groups

Interpersonal Process/Group Maintenance

- Group identity and individual allegiance
- Group norms and culture
- Feedback processes
- Group-process roles
- Conflict-resolution methods
- Capabilities for coping
- Problem ownership
- Supervisor/subordinate relationships
- Subgroups and coalitions
- Interpersonal and role conflict
- Other interpersonal-process elements (trust, openness, and so forth)

Target Group
- The entire organization

Group Size
- All employees
- Data feedback and discussion in individual work groups
- Intergroup meetings if desired for communication of higher-level decisions

Setting
- Typically on site in conference settings in order to minimize work interruptions

Methods
- A contract session is held to clarify objectives and expectations.
- Questions are developed to survey attitudes about pertinent work issues.
- The survey is administered to all employees at the same time if possible.
- Anonymous results from the survey are compiled into a data package, and copies of the package are made and distributed to all participants.
- Starting at the lowest organizational level, work groups meet to analyze the data.
- Each work group develops action plans to deal with areas of concern that the group can handle.
- Problems requiring more data, coordination, or assistance are referred to the next higher organizational level.
- The members of the higher level develop action plans in conjunction with subordinate problems as well as their own concerns and then communicate their decisions to the lower levels; this process is repeated to the top of the organization.

Rationale for Methods
- Organizational climate can be gauged at a given point in time.
- The survey process offers a relatively quick, efficient method of gathering data on attitudes.
- All work groups, including the least influential, are given an opportunity to review data that are relevant to them; to interpret the positive and negative aspects of the data for themselves; to assess how they compare with the overall organization; and to develop their own plans, requests, and recommendations.

Practitioner Involvement
- Imperative (either internal or external)
- External particularly helpful in early stages to help to motivate the groups and keep them on a problem-solving course

Time Relevance
- Most useful as a follow-up to initial skill-building activities; provides an indication of areas of concern in which other types of interventions may be helpful
- Can be useful as a first step toward OD if prior analysis clearly indicates little suspicion or fear regarding the intentions of higher management and if the organization has not previously misused attitude surveys

SURVEY-GUIDED DEVELOPMENT
ACTION SEQUENCE

1

Contract Session

- Clarifying the characteristics of survey-guided development
- Outlining project objectives and expectations
- Establishing the need for a survey-planning committee

2

Survey Planning

- Selecting appropriate dimensions and questions for the survey

3

Survey Administration

- Administering the survey to all participants

4

Consolidation of Data

- Processing survey results
- Preparing data packages for all participants

5

Training of Work-Group Supervisors

- Teaching supervisors how to conduct survey-feedback meetings with their subordinates and how to help subordinates respond to data

6

Feedback Meetings

- Distributing and discussing data packages in each work group
- Clarifying relevant group issues
- Dealing with issues within the group's control
- Making suggestions on issues beyond the group's control for referral to higher levels

7

Review of Items Referred Upward

- Determining appropriate responses to suggestions submitted by lower-level groups

8

Development of a Communication Strategy

- Establishing a beneficial method of conveying decisions made in the previous step

9

Communication of Decisions

- Conveying decisions via the method determined in step 8

10

Assessment

- Surveying participant reactions to the intervention

SURVEY-GUIDED DEVELOPMENT
OPERATING PROCEDURE

1. *Contract Session*

   This is a preliminary planning session involving the practitioner and appropriate members of the organization's management. Its purpose is to establish a clear understanding of the characteristics of *survey-guided development*, which is an ongoing, interactive process that is data based, goal oriented, educational, work-group centered, and designed to accomplish the following objectives:

   - To involve as many system members as possible in OD;
   - To identify status-quo conditions in each work group as well as management problems and action opportunities; and
   - To generate data about needed improvements and to develop action plans to effect these improvements, with primary emphasis on responsibility at the lowest possible level.

   With this definition in mind, the practitioner and the management group outline an acceptable strategic plan for the intervention, surfacing concerns and mutual expectations regarding logistics, commitment, costs, and so forth. To achieve the best possible results, however, minimal "ground rules" should be established at the outset; instead, the management group should be asked to establish a survey-planning committee to function in the next step.

2. *Survey Planning*

   The practitioner and the survey-planning committee meet to design a survey tailored to the specific needs and characteristics of the organization. Although pre-existing surveys may be used as references, survey-guided development is more action than research oriented. The purpose of composing and using the survey is as follows:

   - To provide opportunities to generate commitment to and motivation for specific corrective action throughout the system at the lowest level possible;
   - To close the gap between the real and the ideal situations; and
   - To help build into the system a capacity and framework for solving problems and creating opportunities affecting overall organizational performance and the quality of work life.

   Thus, the survey should be designed to accommodate the organization as seen by the members of the survey-planning committee. The practitioner should point out the following difficulties typically encountered when composing a survey:

   - Questions with admittedly multiple meanings;
   - Assumptions about questions;
   - Lack of a clear-cut choice of appropriate improvement actions;
   - Selection of an appropriate model for use in data analysis; and
   - Various issues connected with validity, raised expectations, and so forth.

   The design emphasis should be on clarity, relevance, simplicity, and the eventual ability to identify data according to specific work group. Attention should also be given to identifying work groups whose data should be combined for consideration (see step 4).

After the survey has been designed, the committee must determine a method for its administration. The method chosen should be one that is unlikely to inhibit candor or to induce fear of reprisal for honesty. In addition, scheduling realities and related constraints must be considered.

3. *Survey Administration*

Ideally, all employees should complete the survey. In the course of giving the participants instructions for completing the survey, the practitioner should explain that subsequently they will be participating in separate work-group meetings to review results and to engage in planning and generating recommendations in response to the data that are applicable to their individual work groups.

4. *Consolidation of Data*

A well-designed survey lends itself to easy processing of data, yielding computations that can be readily transferred into simple bar graphs and charts for use during the feedback process. In addition, the practitioner should prepare a data package with contents as follows:

- All actual responses or representative responses, without speaker identification, for each survey category;
- An overall summary of the data;
- A summary of each work group's data; and
- Additional sets of data reflecting certain combinations of work groups (as deemed useful by the survey-planning committee).

After the data package has been prepared, a copy should be made for each participant.

5. *Training of Work-Group Supervisors*

All work-group supervisors undergo three to five hours of training in planning and conducting a survey-feedback meeting with their immediate subordinates. The practitioner should explain that the feedback meetings are the key to the success of the intervention. In each meeting the survey results are shared, and the group's work processes are analyzed in light of the survey results as well as data contributed by the participants. The meetings start with the topmost organizational team and progress downward through the organizational hierarchy. The primary objective of such a meeting is to plan appropriate action to be taken by the group in response to the survey results. The first phase of the process of responding is to determine a course of activity for each item within the work group's control. The second phase involves an information flow from the lower levels to the upper levels. The members identify issues over which they have no control; generate ideas and suggestions concerning related causes, effects, and recommendations; and submit the results of their work to the next higher level. The members of the next higher level, in turn, either act on these items or refer them to an even higher level for response.

The time schedule for such a meeting should be discussed with the supervisors. The following agenda is set up for a two-hour period, the minimum amount of time required. It is recommended, however, that each supervisor allot three to four hours in case subordinates want or need more time to discuss the data or to plan action in accordance with these data.

1. Reporting survey results *(fifteen minutes)*
2. Clarifying issues connected with the results *(one hour)*
3. Dealing with issues within the control of the group and planning further sessions to finalize plans as needed *(thirty minutes)*
4. Surfacing and making suggestions concerning issues beyond the group's control *(ten minutes)*
5. Committing to a follow-up review of actions taken *(five minutes)*

In addition to discussing the content and scheduling of the feedback meetings, the practitioner should conduct training that incorporates the following subjects and skills:

- Survey-guided development as a process;
- The importance of survey feedback to this process;
- Preparation for the meeting (analyzing survey data, using a third party to assist, determining key areas of concern, identifying issues over which the group has control and those over which it has no control, and so forth);
- Ways to start the meeting (by clarifying "ground rules," the role of the third party, ways in which the data will be discussed, objectives of the meeting, and confidentiality);
- Problem identification (identifying and posting, objectifying, categorizing, determining priorities, differentiating cause from effect, and avoiding premature solutions;)
- Problem solving (brainstorming, establishing criteria, planning action steps, and determining sequences of steps); and
- General skills (dealing with resistance and/or silence, "gatekeeping" or encouraging participation and suggestions, summarizing, giving effective feedback, and handling conflicts or misunderstandings).

The involvement of a third party such as the practitioner to assist in facilitating such a meeting is recommended, but supervisors should not be compelled to allow the presence of an outsider. Instead, they should be exposed to the benefits of involving a third party, such as greater openness and risk taking, as well as the possible risks, such as the development of perceptions that undermine the supervisor's image with the group or dependency. After the benefits and risks have been clarified, the supervisors should be allowed to make their own decisions.

6. *Feedback Meetings*

During this step feedback meetings take place as explained in detail in the previous step.

7. *Review of Items Referred Upward*

As discussed in step 5, part of the process of a feedback meeting is to generate data and recommendations regarding issues over which the work group has no control. During this step all such information is referred to higher-level work groups. Ideally, when this happens only those items that cannot be dealt with are forwarded to still higher levels; this approach allows the top management team to devote its attention exclusively to items that require its specific authority. Sometimes a higher-level group receives items that the originating group can deal with but is unaware that it may do so; in this case such items should be returned with appropriate explanations and reassurances.

Higher-level work groups typically receive the following types of items:

- Expressions of concern without solutions;
- Recommendations for specific action to correct perceived problems; and
- Requests for approval to take action.

Each of these items should be reviewed, and one of the following responses should be made:

- Development of an action plan to address the item;
- Notification that action cannot be taken for specific reasons; or
- Approval or disapproval of a particular request, either with or without modification, for specific reasons.

To make the appropriate decision on an item, the members of a higher-level team may need to request that the work-group supervisor enlighten them regarding any perceived ambiguities. Care should be taken that such a discussion is constructive in tone. In addition, care should be taken to avoid wasting time during this decision-making process by second-guessing the group's reaction or denying the reality or importance of an item. Ground rules about such matters should be established in advance.

8. *Development of a Communication Strategy*

After the higher-level groups have determined responses to all items, thought should be given to a strategy for conveying these decisions. Sending a memorandum, for example, generally has a far less beneficial effect than a brief, face-to-face meeting attended by the work group and a management representative. The practitioner should emphasize that this is an excellent opportunity to establish meaningful communications among organizational members who are often widely separated from each other and that failing to capitalize on this opportunity may undermine the entire intervention.

9. *Communication of Decisions*

This step consists of the actual implementation of the communication strategy developed in the previous step. If meetings are deemed appropriate to convey decisions, they need not be lengthy, but should be planned with group-process principles in mind and with a meaningful exchange as the goal. Obviously, higher management cannot always reply with the hoped-for answer; the manner in which any answer is given, however, can have a lasting effect that is either positive or negative.

10. *Assessment*

The authors recommend that a brief survey of employee reaction to the overall process be made at this point. This practice not only reassures employees of management's genuine interest; it also produces reactions that can benefit the organization in subsequent efforts of this type. Survey questions should be focused on the quality of the survey instrument, the work-group meetings, follow-through to date, and responses from higher levels.

NEW-PLANT START-UP
OVERVIEW

Objectives
- To ensure the implementation of a comprehensive, multifaceted organizational plan to meet identified start-up goals
- To foster among employees a high level of ownership and commitment to organizational principles and characteristics that are likely to meet technical, social, and cost/profit objectives
- To help to coordinate social and technical systems within the plant, thereby ensuring cohesiveness, collaboration, motivation, and a balanced use of resources

Focus

Task
- Overall organizational performance as a function of design
- Long- and short-range organizational goals, characteristics, and priorities
- Organizational structure, operating procedures, and performance efficiency
- The balance between technical- and human-resource utilization to achieve optimum effectiveness and interaction
- Individual and group performance planning and implementation

Group Maintenance
- Organizational norms, values, and related characteristics
- Role expectations, clarification, and development
- Systems development
- Capabilities for coping, multilevel and intergroup feedback, cooperation, trust, climate, and conflict management
- Congruency among individual, group, and organizational values

Target Group
- The organization's management
- Other employee groups involved in plant design and start-up

Group Size
- All managers if possible; if not, representatives from as many functional groups and organizational levels as practical
- All members of other work groups participating in start-up
- Limited only by constraints of scheduling, number of personnel involved during early planning stages, and so forth

Setting
- Dictated by start-up facility circumstances
- Off site desirable, but on site suitable if the participants can be free from outside disturbances

Methods	• The practitioner and the management meet for a preliminary planning session.
	• The practitioner and the top management group meet to develop a strategic plan detailing key events and the sequence of these events.
	• A determination is made regarding specific systems characteristics that are consistent with plant objectives.
	• Further planning takes place to ensure that the design and development of the technical and social systems are consistent with plant objectives and systems characteristics.
	• Team-building sessions are conducted at all management levels to ensure both group and intergroup effectiveness.
	• All participating managers meet to establish the policies and practices that will govern organizational behavior.
	• Individual jobs are designed.
	• Employee-training and -orientation sessions are held.
	• Various issues and concerns are explored after start-up to ensure that the implementation of systems has been consistent with plans and values.
Rationale for Methods	• Effective plant designing includes consideration of human-resource utilization.
	• Failure to integrate sociotechnical dynamics during start-up planning and implementation can lead to serious problems.
	• Organizational members can best develop in and become behaviorally committed to a system that they themselves have designed.
	• The planning of organizational characteristics should occur prior to the designing of technical systems.
	• If personnel are required to implement nontraditional systems, they should be involved in the development of these systems.
	• Systems that meet goals related to cost, quality, and productivity do not simply happen; they result from joint planning, a clear understanding of expectations, and development of teams that function and interact effectively.
Practitioner Involvement	• Critical for actual intervention; desirable for first few progress reviews, with management eventually assuming responsibility for follow-up
Time Relevance	• The initiating events during the planning and development of a new plant
	• Periodic follow-up sessions as required

NEW-PLANT START-UP
ACTION SEQUENCE

1

Preliminary Planning

- Developing initial agreements regarding the scope of the project, the nature of the processes to be employed, the role of the practitioner, and timing

2

Strategic Planning

- Developing an organizational-mission statement
- Listing strengths and weaknesses
- Establishing an overview of the project
- Identifying key planning objectives
- Developing related action plans and assignments

3

Organization and Systems Development

- Listing system characteristics that are consistent with organizational values and objectives
- Listing beliefs about people that are consistent with system characteristics, values, and objectives

4

Technical-System Development

- Planning technical systems that are consistent with earlier plans and decisions (involving outside resources as necessary)

5

Strategic-Planning Update

- Reviewing planning to date (presentation from top managers to middle managers)
- Providing an opportunity for middle managers to offer input and to increase ownership

6

Team Building (Top Management)

- Exploring experience to date as a team
- Making related plans to improve effectiveness

7

Management-Practices Seminar

- Meeting to establish management practices and policies consistent with plans and decisions made thus far (all managers)

8

Team Building (Middle and Lower Management)

- Exploring team experience to date
- Making plans to enhance effectiveness and ensure congruency

9

Job Development

- Developing job content and structure consistent with systems characteristics and sociotechnical principles

10

Problem-Solving Training for Skilled Workers

- Teaching problem identification and solution to skilled workers to enhance their contributions and participation

11

Orientation of Unskilled Workers

- Orienting unskilled workers as to systems characteristics and related objectives (as part of their training)

12

Operating-Issue Census

- Exploring issues and concerns related to implementation of start-up plans (all personnel)
- Setting dates for follow-up sessions as deemed necessary

NEW-PLANT START-UP
OPERATING PROCEDURE

1. *Preliminary Planning*

This step is critical to the ultimate scope and success of an organizational start-up project. During the planning session the project is defined in terms of the organization, the experience of the practitioner, and economic and logistical issues. At the outset the authors generally explain their values concerning the integration of human- and technical-systems characteristics with the processes necessary for related planning and development. In turn, the managers who are present should be encouraged to ask questions and state their concerns so that misunderstandings can be avoided.

It has been the authors' experience that new plant managers often postpone involving a practitioner until far too many technical aspects of the project have already been determined and set in place. Unfortunately, such aspects are likely to have a profoundly negative effect on the subsequent dynamics occurring between the social and technical systems. This likelihood is due to the fact that historically start-up patterns have been based on the assumption that human resources are essentially an adjunct to technology rather than the prime mover thereof. Thus, the planning of this intervention should take place as early as possible in the life cycle of a new organizational unit.

The verbal contracting that occurs during this session must ensure that the client managers present understand the scope of the project, the nature of the processes to be employed and the rationale for them, the mutual expectations implicit in the contract in terms of resource commitment, their own roles and the practitioner's role, the necessity for support from the larger system of which the start-up unit is a part, and scheduling and timing. Agreeing on all of these points at this time enables the practitioner to commit the various understandings to writing for later reference as necessary. This is particularly important when all of the management personnel who will ultimately participate are not yet involved.

2. *Strategic Planning*

The purpose of this event is to help the top management group to develop and/or confirm a two- to three-year strategic plan for the start-up, ensuring ownership of and commitment to its implementation. Following the format, content, and rationale of the intervention in this chapter entitled "Strategic Planning," the top management group develops an organizational-mission statement; lists known strengths and weaknesses associated with mission accomplishment; identifies key operational restraints and environmental arenas that are likely to affect the start-up; lists critical facts and assumptions associated with each restraint and arena; identifies specific goals and objectives required to respond to all factors; and then develops preliminary action plans to ensure accomplishment of each goal and objective, including timing and assignments.

After the action plans have been written, it is important that each manager receive copies of them and that dates be established for progress reviews. Care should be taken to ensure against overscheduling and to allow for unexpected delays. Managers should be encouraged to take a conservative approach when establishing target dates to avoid later discouragement and a loss of commitment associated with missing deadlines. At this point it is difficult for most management teams to predict accurately the number and nature of problems that are likely to interfere with plan implementation, and many managers also tend to be overly ambitious despite disclaimers to the contrary.

3. *Organization and Systems Development*

This step consists of developing a list of ideal characteristics that the top management team envisions for the unit to be created. These characteristics should be consistent with the strategic plan developed in step 2. Then the group determines the values and beliefs inherent in these characteristics and defines them in writing. The elements defined generally include the following:

- The organizational structure, including the number and types of anticipated functions, the design and content of critical positions or jobs within the structure, hoped-for interrelationships across organizational boundaries, and criteria for membership to serve as guidelines for recruitment;
- Beliefs about people at work;
- The basic management philosophy of the planning group; and
- The "givens" in the anticipated social, geophysical, and market environment within which the organizational unit is to be established.

Most management teams find it easier to accomplish this task when they are provided with sample lists of characteristics, values, and beliefs from which they can begin to select, modify, eliminate, and expand. If handled with caution, such lists do not diminish ultimate ownership of the final products, but do help the participants to avoid wasting time in getting started. The ultimate products should represent a broad spectrum of opinions within which the managers may, with the practitioner's help, negotiate a consensus position with which they are comfortable. The practitioner should not hesitate to challenge, confront, and otherwise stimulate discussion at this point because the resulting participant interaction serves to cement relationships that are necessary for effective work in the future and to facilitate the practitioner's own credibility and membership.

4. *Technical-System Development*

At this point the management team turns its attention to the technical system necessary for the new unit being created. It is very important that the technical system be both supportive of and supported by the overall social system that will direct and control it. Often technology is allowed to become king in the organizational environment; planners inadvertently concentrate on state-of-the-art technical developments with little or no focus on the consequences for and impact on employees. The results frequently undermine even the most thoughtful planning for an effective quality of work life within the system. The standards developed during steps 2 and 3, therefore, should be carefully applied to all plans for the establishment of the technical system to ensure congruency and compatibility.

Adopting this sociotechnical-systems approach may necessitate involving engineers, outside vendors, and other internal and external resources. Multidisciplinary, ad-hoc teams that include personnel with technical, systems, and organization-development credentials may be created to review ongoing or as yet undeveloped plans and purchases so that congruency can be achieved and maintained.

5. *Strategic-Planning Update*

In a session attended by top and middle managers, the top management group formally reviews the content of the strategic plan developed in step 2. The purpose of this review is to involve and increase plan ownership at the middle-management level and to make any necessary mid-course corrections and modifications to reflect interim events and experience. Also, because many of these unforeseen factors tend to delay progress and, therefore, to produce inertia, this session is critical in terms of renewing the energy and commitment necessary for follow-through.

6. *Team Building (Top Management)*

By this time the members of the top management group have probably had sufficient time together to be able to benefit from a session conducted according to the intervention entitled "Team Building" in Chapter 5. Data are collected regarding various dimensions of the start-up process and related group dynamics. During this session the practitioner helps the participants to explore the following subjects:

- How well they have worked together to date as a relatively new management group;
- How consistent their individual and group behaviors are with the values and characteristics developed earlier; and
- How they evaluate their decision making, communications, problem solving, and other team skills.

Commitments are made as a result of their evaluations. In addition, a valuable by-product of this session is a high level of enthusiasm for using the team-building process at other organizational levels.

7. *Management-Practices Seminar*

All participating managers from all levels attend a seminar to determine the practical operational implications of the guidelines developed thus far. Considerable give-and-take should be built into this seminar because policies and practices that will govern behavior in the organization are established at this time.

Managers bring years of conditioned responses to new assignments like the ones in question. Because of their conditioning, it is unrealistic to expect them to adapt overnight to a new organizational culture; instead, they must be given time to adjust to ensure structure-wide congruency in leadership behavior. Thus, the seminar should be designed to facilitate in-depth discussion of the basic value system that has been developed and ways to translate this system in terms of leadership style, direction, control, use of power, conflict management, delegation, and so forth.

8. *Team Building (Middle and Lower Management)*

This phase consists of a series of team-building sessions patterned after the one described in step 6. These sessions start with the management group immediately below the top and progress downward through the management structure to involve lower-level groups that are working toward the same objectives. In addition to enhancing team functioning, the sessions tend to reinforce the outcomes emerging from the management-practices seminar in practical ways, strengthening work groups and ensuring learning transfer to "back-home" situations. Ultimately, the series is a system-wide experience that is likely to reinforce the cultural values developed during the previous steps.

9. *Job Development*

At this point an ad-hoc team including representatives from appropriate groups, levels, and disciplines approaches job design from a sociotechnical standpoint. Incorporating the results of steps 3 and 4, this team systematically designs job structures in a manner that increases the probability of improved motivation among incumbent employees, general job satisfaction, and quality of work performance. The team brainstorms lists of tasks related to the ideal unit characteristics established in step 3; categorizes them into key sources of variance from the desired work process; and lists possible variance-control options, which are screened and grouped into logical work modules and related accountabilities for incumbents. Finally, a plan is developed for experimental implementation of the resultant jobs, including orientation and training.

10. *Problem-Solving Training for Skilled Workers*

In this step technicians and skilled craftspeople are trained in problem solving in order to enhance the probability of effective involvement and contributions on their part. This training includes techniques and methods for recognizing problems, specifying deviations, determining possible causes, testing causes, establishing objectives for solution, assessing the adverse consequences of solutions, anticipating potential problems and causes, and developing contingency actions and controls. All techniques that are taught should be consistent with the unit characteristics and job structures previously established.

11. *Orientation of Unskilled Workers*

Unskilled workers should also receive appropriate orientation to the unit characteristics and management practices and policies developed earlier. This orientation should be an integral part of relevant technical training in job content. After a group of such workers has undergone orientation and has achieved a specified level of demonstrated performance, it is a good idea to consider asking selected members of this group to train and orient employees hired in the future. In the authors' experience, supervisors do not always make the most effective trainers because newly hired employees are often reluctant to admit ignorance, anxiety, and lack of understanding to members of management.

12. *Operating-Issue Census*

This step occurs a few weeks after operational start-up and is primarily an attempt to isolate and discuss the problems in the system as designed. The intervention entitled "Issue Census" in Chapter 5 is used for this process. Both management and nonmanagement personnel from all levels of the organization meet to examine issues associated with the actual start-up versus the planned operation. This discussion not only surfaces problems in the application of principles and implementation of systems but also facilitates development of plans to correct and resolve these problems before they become major hindrances to the success of the start-up project. In addition, this process provides a significant vehicle for reinforcing system-wide cooperation and ensuring the establishment of both vertical and horizontal channels of communication early in the project life cycle. Appropriate commitments to follow-up sessions may also be made at this time.

JOB DEVELOPMENT
OVERVIEW

Objectives
- To identify components of a specific job that underutilize talent and/or demotivate incumbents
- To systematically redesign the work involved in a manner that increases the probability of improved incumbent motivation, general job satisfaction, and quality of work performance

Focus

Task
- Impact of job content on individual performance
- Impact of technology on job content
- Motivational potential of existing job tasks and characteristics
- Degree to which the job necessitates skill utilization
- Sources of negative variance in desired performance
- Specific task-structure options for control of negative performance variance
- Specific conditions that foster self-motivation

Individual/Group Maintenance
- Employee ownership and commitment to planned change
- Increased acceptance of change
- The degree to which the work is meaningful to an incumbent
- Personal responsibility for work outcomes
- Job satisfaction

Target Group
- A job-design committee consisting of all employees in the organization who hold the job in question as well as their supervisors

Group Size
- Typically six to eight participants (committee members)

Setting
- On site, with provisions made for interrupted work

Duration
- Typically half-day sessions weekly for two to three months, depending on job complexity

Methods
- The members of the job-design committee are introduced to the principles of job development.
- The committee develops a job-purpose statement and determines the key accountabilities associated with the job.
- The target system, its operations, and related systems are identified; then a diagram is drawn to illustrate the flow of the work performed in all of these systems.
- Ideas are generated regarding ways to increase feedback about performance, to increase autonomy, to complete entire tasks, and to deal with barriers to task accomplishment.
- All ideas are screened according to specific criteria.
- The ideas that have been retained are incorporated into a final job description.
- A plan for training and orienting new employees is designed, and potential problems resulting from the job description are determined.

Rationale for Methods
- Only certain jobs can be meaningfully and productively changed.
- Those best qualified to redesign jobs are incumbents and their supervisors.
- Employees will accept changes when they are involved or represented in change development.
- Both psychological and technological needs must be addressed in meaningful work design.

Practitioner Involvement
- Imperative
- Advisable to include an internal practitioner and an external practitioner to ensure continuity and follow-through

Time Relevance
- Conducted when evidence suggests the existence of problems related to job content

JOB DEVELOPMENT
ACTION SEQUENCE

1
Orientation of Job-Design Committee

- Introducing the members of the job-design committee to basic principles of job development

2
Development of a Job-Purpose Statement

- Writing a statement that specifies the reason for the job's existence

3
Identification of Key Accountabilities

- Determining the end results or desired conditions for which an incumbent is responsible

4
Identification of Systems and Operations

- Identifying the target system
- Describing the operations of that system
- Identifying related systems
- Developing a flow diagram of work performed in all of these systems

5
Brainstorming of Job Dimensions

- Generating ideas for increasing feedback about performance and for increasing autonomy
- Generating ways to complete entire tasks and determining ways to deal with barriers to accomplishing these tasks

6
Screening of Data

- Selecting and eliminating brainstormed items according to specific criteria

7
Development of Final Job Description

- Listing items retained after screening
- Grouping items into work modules
- Comparing items with the purpose statement and the key accountabilities
- Developing an integrated job description

8
Development of Training Program

- Establishing an action plan for training and orienting new employees
- Listing problems that might be encountered with the job description

JOB DEVELOPMENT
OPERATING PROCEDURE

1. *Orientation of Job-Design Committee*

The authors' approach to job development is based on the creation of a job-design committee whose members are responsible for implementing this intervention. Before the committee members attempt to follow these steps, however, they should be introduced to information on the following subjects:*

- Employees and work in today's world (changing expectations, worker profiles, and values about working);
- The relationship between job satisfaction and productivity; and
- Principles of job development.

When presenting such information, the practitioner should be careful not to effect a "data overload." Most job-design committees can function at a comfortable level after learning basic principles and theory.

2. *Development of a Job-Purpose Statement*

The committee writes a purpose statement for the job under consideration. Essentially, this statement should clarify the reason for the existence of the job.

3. *Identification of Key Accountabilities*

In this step the committee determines the job's major accountabilities, which are the end results or the desired conditions for which an incumbent is answerable after a specified length of time. When clarifying this task, the practitioner should emphasize that the committee members are not to list the activities or processes whereby specific results or conditions are obtained.

4. *Identification of Systems and Operations*

The committee first identifies the target system (the functional unit or department) within which the job exists and then describes the basic operations that take place within that system. Such operations include those that effect changes in the state of certain materials or products as well as those that constitute services rendered (by people or machines or both).

The next phase of this step consists of identifying other organizational systems that are related to the target system in the following ways:

- Those that input materials, products, and/or information to the target system (*suppliers*); and
- Those to which the target system outputs materials, products, and/or information (*users*).

---

*A good source for this information is J.R. Hackman and G.R. Oldham, "A New Strategy for Job Enrichment," *California Management Review*, 1975, *17*(4), 57-70.

After identification has been completed, the committee develops a simple work-flow diagram that reflects the sequence of tasks performed in the target and related systems.

5. *Brainstorming of Job Dimensions*

To generate ideas in this step, the committee uses the technique of brainstorming. Rules for using this technique are stipulated by the practitioner as follows:

- Ideas are to be suggested quickly and recorded without any regard whatsoever for practicality and feasibility.
- Reactions to ideas, either favorable or unfavorable, are not permitted.
- The only permitted input following a given suggestion is another idea.

The committee's first brainstorming assignment is to produce as many ideas as possible regarding practices that would enable an incumbent to receive direct, immediate, and regular feedback about the results of his or her efforts. Examples include the following:

- Establishing direct relationships with users in related systems;
- Making the incumbent or the incumbent's supervisor responsible for quality control;
- Providing the incumbent with summaries of performance records;
- Supplying the incumbent with computer reports or other "automated" types of information that are often inaccessible in other forms; and
- Removing barriers that block the incumbent's access to existing information about work performance.

Then the committee brainstorms as many ideas as possible regarding ways to give an incumbent freedom, independence, and discretion in scheduling work and/or determining how he or she will carry out responsibilities. Examples include the following:

- Permitting the incumbent to determine his or her own work hours and break schedule;
- Allowing the incumbent discretion in assigning priorities;
- Authorizing the incumbent to select a way to verify the quality of his or her work; and
- Encouraging the incumbent to seek solutions to problems independent of his or her supervisor, consulting with other members of the organization as necessary.

Next the committee generates as many ideas as possible for enabling an incumbent to complete "whole," identifiable tasks from beginning to end. Each of these tasks should have a visible outcome. Some of the ideas produced might include ways in which existing, fractionalized tasks can be combined to form new and larger modules of work.*

As the final brainstorming assignment, the committee determines ways to control, regulate, or eliminate the barriers to accomplishing the identified tasks, thereby increasing autonomy, task identity, and skill variety while simultaneously contributing to quality, efficiency, and productivity.

---

*It may be helpful at this point to review the work-flow diagram developed in step 4.

6. *Screening of Data*

The committee screens the ideas brainstormed during step 5, selecting and eliminating items by answering the following questions for each:

1. Does the item potentially have to do with task or job *content* or merely the context or environment in which the job is performed?
2. Is the item *concrete* and *specific* or merely a generality?
3. Will the item create conditions for *self-motivation* in one or more of the following ways?
   - By increasing experienced meaningfulness (via skill variety, task identity, or task significance);
   - By improving experienced responsibility for work outcomes (via increased autonomy); or
   - By enhancing knowledge of actual work results (via feedback).
4. Will the item increase an incumbent's *autonomy* in one or more of the following ways?
   - By helping him or her to identify a barrier to task completion;
   - By helping him or her to control, regulate, or eliminate the barrier; or
   - By giving him or her the authority to act on knowledge gained.
5. Will the item be *cost effective?*
   - What might be the payoff to the company?
   - What problems might be encountered with it?
   - How and by whom could these problems be resolved?

7. *Development of Final Job Description*

The committee lists the items retained as a result of the screening process and categorizes these items into logical work modules as appropriate. The results are compared with the purpose statement and with the related accountabilities to ensure consistency. Finally, the committee develops an integrated job description that fits whatever format is currently in use in the organization.

8. *Development of Training Program*

The committee establishes an action plan for leading new employees through training and orientation with regard to the newly developed job. One helpful approach to this task is to produce a check list consisting of the steps that are determined to be necessary. The training program should account for individual differences in ability, experience, and growth needs.

It is also a good idea to list problems that are likely to be encountered. Composing this list helps the committee to avoid ignoring issues associated with differences in the content of the new job versus that of similar jobs in similar organizations.

ROLE DEVELOPMENT
OVERVIEW

Objectives
- To clarify the definitions and expectations of a specific role
- To identify the obligations of the interdependent members of a work group
- To resolve conflict associated with role confusion and ambiguity

Focus

Task

- Definitions of the focal role
- Expectations of others regarding behavior associated with the focal role
- Development of a consensus regarding individual accountabilities and related authority
- Surfacing of role and territorial issues with the intent of negotiating resolutions
- Group definition and delineation of role requirements

Interpersonal/Group Maintenance

- Individual identity within the group
- Resolution of interpersonal conflict about roles
- Interpersonal competence building
- Group ownership and commitment
- Role identity and allegiance
- Group-process roles

Target Group
- A natural work group (supervisor and subordinates)
- Groups that interact with the principal work group (optional)

Group Size
- All members of the work group
- Members of interacting groups as desired

Setting
- On site (unless employed as a segment of another intervention being conducted off site)

Duration
- Two to three days

Methods	• The practitioner and members of the work group meet to discuss and plan the intervention.
	• The total group of participants selects a specific role for examination.
	• The focal role is analyzed to determine the rationale for its existence, its contribution to the group and to organizational goals, its accountabilities, and its typical duties and behaviors.
	• The incumbent in the focal role describes what he or she expects from those in other roles in order to fulfill the focal role; discussion ensues until a consensus is reached regarding legitimate expectations.
	• Those in other roles describe what they expect from the focal role; these comments are discussed until a consensus is reached regarding legitimate expectations.
	• The incumbent is asked to write a role profile, which is discussed and ultimately approved during a follow-through session.
Rationale for Methods	• Interpersonal tension and conflict are often the result of role ambiguity.
	• To minimize or avoid role conflict within a work group, the members need to share their expectations of each other and agree on their role definitions.
	• A work group's culture exerts a significant influence on the behavior of all of its members, regardless of the job descriptions involved.
	• Co-workers are likely to be more supportive of an incumbent in a role that they clearly understand.
Probable Content	• One day for the contract session
	• One to two days for the actual intervention, with approximately half of the time spent in surfacing role definitions and expectations and the rest spent in related negotiation, clarification, and modification of a given role as interpreted by the participants
Practitioner Involvement	• Imperative initially, but the group may be able to function independently during the follow-through session and any subsequent role-development interventions
Time Relevance	• Follows other interventions in which role conflict or confusion is identified as a key issue
	• Excellent follow-up to interventions for new-team start-up, transition planning, new-plant start-up, and job development

ROLE DEVELOPMENT
ACTION SEQUENCE

1

Contract Session

- Meeting with appropriate work-group members to discuss and plan the intervention

2

Focal-Role Selection

- Determining the specific role to be examined and developed

3

Focal-Role Analysis

- Analyzing the purpose, accountabilities, and duties of the focal role

4

Identification of Incumbent's Expectations

- Determining what the incumbent expects of those in interacting roles
- Achieving agreement on legitimate expectations

5

Identification of Others' Expectations

- Determining what those in interacting roles expect from the focal role
- Achieving agreement on legitimate expectations
- Comparing final expectations with those established in step 4

6

Role-Profile Development

- Incorporating all data into a profile of the focal role (prepared by the incumbent after the meeting)

7

Follow-Through Session

- Meeting to review and approve the incumbent's role profile

ROLE DEVELOPMENT
OPERATING PROCEDURE

1. *Contract Session*

The practitioner meets with appropriate members of the work group in which role conflict or confusion has been identified as an issue. During this meeting the practitioner describes the basic process to be followed, answering questions and assisting the work-group members in establishing particulars such as the time and setting of the intervention.

It is important for the practitioner to point out that the purpose of this intervention is not to develop a "job description" for given individuals for use in evaluating or in determining compensation; rather, it is to clarify role parameters within which an incumbent is or should be operating. This process is undertaken with a view toward minimizing misunderstandings and conflict associated with activities in which the incumbent typically engages. The practitioner should also explain that the value of this intervention is that it offers a work group a nonthreatening, supportive setting in which to examine the mutual expectations, demands, and responsibilities of its interdependent members. By engaging in collaborative role analysis and definition, all parties concerned become committed to the role as defined and clarified. Thus, the potential for the development of future concerns about what the incumbent is doing or is supposed to be doing is minimized.

At this time the work-group members might want to consider including members of interdependent groups as participants in the intervention.* If they decide to involve members of other groups, it is especially important during contracting to establish ground rules and an agreed-on agenda process; otherwise, the intervention may give rise to tension, such as that which occurs when the incumbent in the focal role feels that he or she is being forced to justify the existence of the role rather than asked to clarify its components and expectations.

2. *Focal-Role Selection*

The first step of the intervention meeting attended by all participants is to agree on a rationale for selecting a given role on which to focus. This forces the group to explore role-ambiguity issues that may not have been fully surfaced during the event that led to the decision to engage in role development. Also, considerable discomfort, ambiguity, and confusion are avoided by allowing the entire group to decide which role should be examined. (If it is determined that several roles require analysis and clarification, a separate intervention should be scheduled for each of these roles.)

3. *Focal-Role Analysis*

The practitioner invites everyone present to participate in accomplishing the following:

- Developing a purpose statement for the role. The participants write one or two sentences explaining the rationale for the existence of the role in the organization.

---

*This approach is particularly useful, for example, during intergroup team building when a role-conflict issue is surfaced and a plan is developed to deal with it.

- Determining the accountabilities associated with this purpose. Accountabilities are the specific end results or desired conditions for which the role incumbent is held answerable after a given time. (The participants should be cautioned to avoid describing activities; the incumbent's behavior and typical duties are not in question at this point. In addition, when the participants determine more than six major accountabilities, the practitioner usually may assume that the "results" being defined are, in fact, either processes or short-term objectives.)
- Clarifying the position that the role occupies in the organization. This position is defined in terms of achieving organizational goals.
- Identifying typical duties and behaviors. The participants describe the tasks and actions in which the incumbent is frequently engaged.

During this process the practitioner records responses on a chalkboard or newsprint. Items are added and/or deleted until all participants are satisfied that the role has been completely defined.

4. *Identification of Incumbent's Expectations*

The incumbent is asked to describe what he or she expects from the other roles represented in the group in order to fulfill the focal role. These descriptions of expectations are recorded by the practitioner and are then discussed, modified, and expanded until a group consensus is reached regarding legitimate expectations. (Failure to reach consensus usually means that specific expectations are perceived as unreasonable in that there is insufficient authority to bring resources to bear or that some participants perceive duplication of activities. In either case the group can usually see what decision must be made to remedy the situation and who the proper authority is to make that decision.)

5. *Identification of Others' Expectations*

The participants whose roles require interaction with the incumbent in the focal role are asked to describe what they expect from the focal role. As instructions are given, the practitioner stresses the importance of concentrating on the role rather than on the incumbent in order to avoid issues associated strictly with personality and style.

All descriptions are recorded by the practitioner and then discussed, modified, and expanded until the entire group achieves consensus regarding legitimate expectations. It is often useful to suggest that the participants categorize their expectations as follows:

- Actions that must be approved by the focal role;
- Situations that require consulting with the focal role;
- Decisions that must be made by the focal role;
- Occasions that require notification of the focal role;
- Activities and/or personnel that require the supervision of the focal role; and
- Activities that must be performed by the focal role.

The resulting expectations are then compared with those established in the previous step to ensure that the various interacting roles represented in the group coordinate as the participants feel that they should.

6. *Role-Profile Development*

At this point sufficient data exist to prepare a role profile. The incumbent undertakes the responsibility of combining all data generated and preparing a draft of the profile for submission to the total group in a separate follow-through meeting (step 7). This approach permits the incumbent to assume control of the profile and yet allows the group to review the results to ensure clarity and consistency with the agreements and understandings that have been reached.

7. *Follow-Through Session*

The total group reconvenes to review and ultimately approve the role profile drafted by the incumbent. The final profile designates the parameters of the incumbent's position within a "role set" consisting of the focal role and those with which it is interdependent.

COMPLEMENTARY TRAINING

Often a practitioner finds that client participants need training in specific knowledge or skills in order to benefit from OD efforts. Sometimes such knowledge or skills are prerequisites to successful OD interventions, whereas on other occasions they are identified as lacking during the course of interventions. Thus, any successful, long-range change strategy such as is often required to meet the objectives of an OD effort must include as options various events designed to provide particular kinds of training.

INTERVENTION CATEGORIES

The training interventions in this chapter are organized as follows:

1. An intervention that is associated with such group dynamics as decision making, problem solving, cooperation, communication, conflict resolution, and so forth:
   * Team-Skills Training

2. An intervention that is related to personal preferences, tendencies, values, and behaviors concerning leadership:
   * Leadership-Style Analysis

3. An intervention that is associated with the nature, objectives, and methodology of organization development:
   * OD Seminar

4. An intervention that concentrates on the impact of racism and increasing multi-cultural diversity on organizational effectiveness:
   * Minority-Awareness Training

5. An intervention that is concerned with the impact of sexism and sex-role stereotyping on organizational effectiveness:
   * Gender-Awareness Training

The particular training intervention selected as well as the time chosen to conduct the intervention depend on the organization; its general state of readiness; its past history of such training, if any; and so forth. Appropriate training sessions may well complement and reinforce other OD interventions, provided that such sessions clearly result from joint analysis and planning. Thus, these training interventions help to overcome the problem with learning transfer that many practitioners encounter when traditional training is not associated with ongoing efforts to change the organizational culture so that it encourages use of the skills and/or knowledge acquired.

TEAM-SKILLS TRAINING
OVERVIEW

Objectives
- To introduce teamwork concepts
- To foster skills, knowledge, and capabilities in group dynamics, group influence and coordination, personal management style, self-assessment, and interpersonal awareness in individual and group relationships

Focus

Task
- Goal setting and strategy
- Problem solving
- Resource utilization
- Creativity
- Coordination
- Influencing

Interpersonal Process
- Trust
- Openness
- Feedback
- Collaboration
- Competition
- Conflict
- Participation
- Risk taking
- Ownership of behavior
- Assumption testing
- Attitudes, perceptions, and feelings

Target Group
- Members of a single work group or peers from groups that either do or do not work together

Group Size
- Limited to twenty-five to thirty participants to achieve maximum effectiveness

Setting
- Off site so that the participants can be free from work interruptions

Duration
- Approximately two and one-half days

Methods	• The practitioner meets with members of management to discuss the objectives, format, and content of the training.
	• At the outset of the training, the participants reveal their feelings and expectations regarding the experience and develop a list of behavioral norms.
	• The practitioner administers instruments to determine the participants' present knowledge and use of team skills, defines the various skills, and presents an overview of the training sessions.
	• Through the means of activities, simulations, discussions, lecturettes, and other instruments, the practitioner conducts training in a variety of team skills.
	• The participants provide each other with information about their behavior during training and discuss ways to apply their learnings.
	• After the participants evaluate the entire experience, the practitioner reinforces the relevance of the training to back-home situations as well as to other OD events being planned.

Rationale for Methods	• The training experience captures complex job conditions in key situations that highlight basic elements of individual, group, and intergroup behavior affecting efforts and performance.
	• The process of analyzing group behavior and activity is expedited.
	• Common OD bonds are built in terms of perception and the terminology of team skills and teamwork.
	• Experiential learning promotes individualized assessment of results and behavior by:

1. Encouraging maximum participation, viewing *active* learning as better than *passive* learning;
2. Allowing for analysis of each event in terms of its work relevance, viewing problem-centered learning as more enduring than theory-based learning;
3. Encouraging individual and group feedback, viewing two-way communication as more helpful to learning than one-way communication; and
4. Allowing the participants to share the responsibility for their learning, thereby limiting the judgments made by the practitioner.

Model of Experiential Learning

Probable Content	• One-half day for the planning meeting
	• Approximately two days (including evenings) for the training sessions: half of the time spent on the introduction and orientation as well as training in teamwork, group decision making and problem solving, values and perceptions, and cooperation and communication; the other half spent on evaluation and reconnection, power and conflict management, intergroup teamwork, feedback and back-home planning, and assessment

Practitioner Involvement	• Imperative

Time Relevance	• A key first step in situations in which the organization is new to OD; conflictual, dysfunctional, or noncooperative behavior is evident; and/or a common understanding and framework are needed to legitimize the introduction or pursuit of other OD interventions

TEAM-SKILLS TRAINING
ACTION SEQUENCE

1	**2**	**3**
Planning Meeting • Meeting with designated members of management to outline content, format, and rationales • Answering related questions • Determining logistics and so forth	**Introduction** • Eliciting feelings and expectations regarding the training experience • Establishing norms • Introducing the concept of experiential learning	**Orientation** • Administering instruments to assess present knowledge and use of team skills • Conducting an activity that introduces and reinforces the need for team skills
4	**5**	**6**
Teamwork • Using an activity, a simulation, or a discussion to reinforce the importance of teamwork in organizations	**Group Decision Making and Problem Solving** • Using an activity and a discussion to expose the participants to the issues of participation and involvement as related to these skills	**Values and Perceptions** • Using a lecturette, a simulation, or an activity to illustrate the ways in which people's value systems affect their perceptions and their behavior in groups
7	**8**	**9**
Cooperation and Communication • Using activities and a discussion to raise group awareness of issues and dynamics involving these skills as applied in group settings	**Evaluation and Reconnection** • Sharing perceptions of the first day of training • Evaluating adherence to established norms	**Power and Conflict Management** • Using an activity, a simulation, and/or a lecturette to treat the issues of power dynamics and conflict management in and between groups
10	**11**	**12**
Intergroup Teamwork • Using a simulation and a discussion to illustrate the ways in which team skills affect intergroup relations	**Feedback and Back-Home Planning** • Using instruments and/or feedback discussions to provide the participants with data concerning their workshop behavior • Developing plans to experiment with new behaviors in back-home situations	**Assessment** • Generating data about the training experience • Relating the training to back-home situations and to other OD events

Complementary Training 141

TEAM-SKILLS TRAINING
OPERATING PROCEDURE

1. *Planning Meeting*

This meeting is required to make decisions regarding logistics and to ensure that the client managers understand and support the objectives, format, and content of the training. Of particular importance is the need to communicate to those attending this meeting that the training is an integral part of a multifaceted effort and not an isolated intervention intended to effect its own changes. This point is emphasized because the authors' experience is that most participants in typical organizations tend to have one or the other of the following misconceptions:

- Unrealistic expectations regarding changes evolving from training; or
- A skeptical if not cynical view of training based on past experiences with unrealized expectations.

Thus, in clarifying the rationale for conducting team-skills training, the practitioner should explain that the knowledge and skills acquired are expected to contribute to the success of other OD events. For example, most groups undergoing team building for the first time benefit greatly from having had team-skills training first.*

2. *Introduction*

This is the initial event for the first day of training, which ideally is held off site in an interruption-free environment. Comfortable chairs should be provided, but it is preferable not to use tables because they often become barriers to communication as well as to free movement. If tables are required for various activities added by the practitioner, they should be placed against walls for use only when appropriate.

To begin the session, the practitioner should use some technique for surfacing the participants' feelings and expectations regarding the training. This procedure enables the practitioner to correct any existing misunderstandings about the intended focus as established during the planning meeting. Then the group should be assisted in developing a list of norms most likely to produce a beneficial learning experience. Finally, the differences between experiential and didactic learning should be clarified, and introductions should take place.

3. *Orientation*

The practitioner should administer one or two instruments designed to gauge the participants' current knowledge and use of team skills.** After the results have been

---

*The ideal application of this kind of training is to lead homogeneous groups through the experience together, providing them with a relatively tension-free and positive environment in which to acquire skills and knowledge. This shared learning experience often gives them a reference point and a base on which to build as they proceed to confront the actual issues that relate to their effectiveness.

**For examples of instruments, activities, and lecturettes, see J.W. Pfeiffer and J.E. Jones (Eds.), *The Annual Handbook for Group Facilitators.* San Diego, CA: University Associates, 1972-1981.

assessed, the next procedure is to conduct a highly involving and enjoyable activity that introduces and reinforces the need for such skills. Hundreds of these abound in the literature available to group facilitators. Depending on the type of activity selected, it may be necessary to restate the rationale for experience-based learning; otherwise, some participants may feel that they are being asked simply to play a game.

The authors prefer to emphasize the practical nature of team skills as distinguished from their philosophical or more abstract features in order to reinforce their relevance to the rest of the training experience as well as to back-home situations. Thus, at this point the practitioner should define various team skills, presenting an overview of the training sessions.

4. Teamwork

To continue reinforcing the importance of teams in organizations, the practitioner leads the participants through an activity, a simulation, or a discussion that concentrates on the relevance of teamwork to typical, everyday situations faced by the participants. This step includes further emphasis on the team skills already outlined: group decision making, group problem solving, value confrontation, giving and receiving personal feedback, cooperation, conflict management, and communication.

5. Group Decision Making and Problem Solving

In this step the practitioner helps the participants to surface and deal with the issues of participation and involvement as they relate to group decision making and problem solving. One way to accomplish this is to conduct an activity that addresses these issues.* The critical discussion following such an activity can provide a foundation for important exchanges during other interventions that may be planned as follow-up to this training. Thus, the participants should be allowed to process their learnings. Although a lengthy processing period may be boring for some participants who find the experience neither new nor impactful, such individuals generally tend to be in the minority. Even those who have participated in the same or a similar activity usually benefit from undergoing the experience with the members of their own work group(s). If the practitioner senses or knows at the outset that some group members have participated in the activity previously, he or she may simply state that all such individuals should participate in any way they see fit without revealing their previous experiences to the others.

6. Values and Perceptions

Through the means of a lecturette, a simulation, or an activity, the practitioner helps the participants to understand the ways in which their value systems affect their perceptions and, thus, their behavior in groups. When introducing this step, care should be taken to avoid conveying to the participants that an attempt is being made to assess, judge, or modify their value systems. The authors find that relating perceptual differences to conflict sources and behavior in group settings is particularly useful as a transition to other steps.

---

*The authors recommend A. Shedlin and W.H. Schmidt, "Hollow Square: A Communications Experiment," in J.W. Pfeiffer and J.E. Jones (Eds.), *A Handbook of Structured Experiences for Human Relations Training*, Vol. II (Rev.). San Diego, CA: University Associates, 1974.

7. *Cooperation and Communication*

It is recommended that the practitioner employ one or two activities that deal with cooperation and communication, the interdependence of these two skills, and the roles that they play in competition and conflict within and between groups. It is particularly important that the participants recognize how frequently a lifetime of conditioning toward competition influences one's ability to cooperate and to communicate openly and honestly. At this point it is a good idea to discuss the back-home implications of learnings. If the participants are from different work groups, each group may discuss these implications separately.

8. *Evaluation and Reconnection*

This event, which starts the second day of training, provides the participants with an opportunity to share perceptions and feelings about the experience of the first day. The participants may also evaluate the degree to which the norms that they established are being adhered to.

The practitioner benefits from the sharing process by ascertaining the participants' levels of insight, which may influence what is emphasized during the second day. In addition, this occasion provides an opportunity to remind the participants of the objectives and goals. The greatest benefit of the procedure, however, is that it helps to prevent the phenomenon of "pluralistic ignorance" that is frequently observed in workshop settings: Individuals assume either that they are alone in their feelings or that almost everyone else shares their feelings. Peer-group input often modifies negative perceptions and reinforces positive ones.

9. *Power and Conflict Management*

Generally by this time a foundation has been laid for the treatment of group conflict and power dynamics so that the practitioner can proceed with an appropriate simulation or activity covering these subjects. Again, many such activities abound in training literature, as do models on conflict management that may provide the content of either introductory or concluding lecturettes.

10. *Intergroup Teamwork*

Much of the program to this point has dealt with typical dynamics associated with the skills either present or absent within a team. The theme for this step is relating and applying these skills to relationships and interaction between groups. An appropriate simulation is conducted and followed by ample time for processing the data generated and relating these data to back-home behavior.

11. *Feedback and Back-Home Planning*

It is particularly useful toward the end of the training experience to facilitate feedback among and between the participants concerning their impact on each other. The use of triads during this step helps to provide ample individual discussion time. Personal sharing of back-home situations and/or commitments to experiment with new behavior is also appropriate while the participants are in subgroups. In addition, simple instruments may be used as a feedback vehicle, provided that the climate is appropriate.

12. Assessment

Although rating sheets are an option for accomplishing evaluation of the training experience, the authors prefer asking the group to share data and then recording and posting these data. In addition to providing an evaluation of the training experience as designed and facilitated by the practitioner, the sharing process allows the participants to assess their own behavior in terms of the norms that they set for themselves. In order to connect the experience to the long-range development strategy under way, the practitioner should make appropriate presentations that help to tie the entire training design to the back-home relevance of team skills and any follow-up events being planned.

LEADERSHIP-STYLE ANALYSIS
OVERVIEW

Objectives
- To provide an opportunity for leaders to examine their own personal preferences, tendencies, and values concerning leadership style
- To increase understanding of the strengths associated with specific, researched styles that are widely employed in dealing with people and problems at work
- To help leaders to explore specific ways in which they may manage, develop, and apply the strengths associated with various styles in their own work environments so that they may increase their leadership effectiveness

Focus

Task
- Personal awareness of the nature, tendencies, and strengths associated with various leadership-behavior styles under both favorable and unfavorable work conditions
- Exploration of the impact of various leadership styles on subordinates and work environments
- Individual self-analysis via instruments and related feedback
- Broadening behavioral options through exposure to alternative leadership styles, specific applications, further development of strengths, and control of style excesses

Interpersonal Process
- Capabilities for coping
- Individual stereotyping
- Stress management
- Assumption testing
- Openness and trust
- Feedback and self-analysis
- Self-awareness
- Conflict management

Target Group
- Leadership peers
- Diagonal segment of administrators, managers, and supervisors
- Management/administrative committees/teams/boards/councils

Group Size
- No more than twenty-four participants so that sufficient attention can be given to individuals

Setting
- Off site desirable, but on site suitable if ample space is provided and the participants can be free from outside disturbances

Duration
- Approximately three full-day sessions for the actual intervention, with time between the sessions to allow for additional thought about personal needs and preferences; sessions should not extend beyond two weeks once begun

Methods	• The participants and the practitioner meet for a preliminary session; the practitioner presents an overview of the intervention, distributes instruments to be completed prior to the first workshop meeting, and gives instructions for instrument completion.
	• The participants meet and are exposed to a basic model of leadership that equips them with a frame of reference and a broad spectrum of styles from which to select.
	• The completed instruments are discussed; then the participants take part in an activity that assists them in understanding their leadership profiles.
	• The theories behind the instruments are explained, and the organizational variables associated with various leadership styles are discussed.
	• The practitioner conducts an experiential activity that illustrates the interconnection of personal needs, value systems, and leadership.
	• Organizational stress is discussed, and fear-producing leader behaviors are identified and analyzed.
	• The value of authentic management is presented.
	• Back-home issues and opportunities are discussed.
	• If the practitioner wishes, the participants give and receive feedback about their personal leadership styles.

Rationale for Methods

- Organizational effectiveness is affected by the leadership style employed by those in positions of influence and control.
- Individual and group performance effectiveness is enhanced by understanding, acceptance, and application of the proven strengths associated with a wide range of leadership styles.
- A setting is provided for supportive, nonthreatening self-analysis regarding specific behaviors associated with leadership patterns.
- Entire leadership hierarchies can examine the consequences of various styles without being influenced to adopt one particular style.
- Individuals and groups are more likely to risk new back-home behaviors if they have shared a common experience concerning leadership.
- If flexible, contingency-based leadership is to develop, individuals and groups need vehicles for increased self-awareness.

Practitioner Involvement

- Mandatory

Time Relevance

- Excellent initiating or follow-up event for team-skills training, team building, or intergroup team building

LEADERSHIP-STYLE ANALYSIS
ACTION SEQUENCE

1
Orientation and Prework

- Reviewing the workshop objectives
- Distributing instruments on leadership style and giving instructions for completion

2
Presentation of Basic Leadership Model

- Presenting a model of leadership based on contingencies
- Introducing the concept of authenticity

3
Consideration of Value Systems

- Discussing the completed instruments and helping the participants to understand their leadership profiles
- Conducting an activity that demonstrates the impact of values on leader behavior

4
Integration of Values and Leadership

- Explaining the theories behind the instruments
- Discussing the organizational variables associated with various leadership styles

5
Experiential Activity

- Conducting an experiential activity that stresses the interconnection of personal needs, value systems, and leadership-style options

6
Discussion of Stress

- Discussing primary sources of organizational stress

7
Analysis of the Consequences of Fear

- Generating data about fear-producing leader behaviors

8
Presentation of Authentic Management

- Presenting the benefits of developing an authentic, unique, and internalized leadership style

9
Reinforcement of Authentic Management

- Conducting experiential activities that illustrate authentic-management theory

10
Discussion of Back-Home Issues and Opportunities

- Discussing in subgroups real-life concerns about style options and related consequences
- Giving and receiving feedback about individual styles (optional)

11
Summary and Conclusion

- Summarizing the key points of the intervention
- Discussing the transfer of learnings to back-home situations
- Evaluating the workshop

LEADERSHIP-STYLE ANALYSIS
OPERATING PROCEDURE

1. *Orientation and Prework*

The authors advocate that the practitioner hold a short prework meeting for the following purposes:

- To review workshop objectives, emphasizing that the focus will be on self-awareness and related style development rather than on advocating a particular leadership style; and
- To distribute copies of selected instruments to be completed and scored individually prior to the first workshop session.

Questions about the presentation and materials should be elicited and answered, and arrangements should be made for orienting participants who are absent from this meeting. At this time scheduling should also be considered. The workshop lends itself well to a Monday-Wednesday-Friday schedule, allowing time between sessions for reflection and energy recovery and for avoidance of "data overload" and fatigue.

Because any benefit derived from a leadership-style instrument is contingent on honest completion, the practitioner should caution the participants not to second-guess the instruments. It is helpful at this point to minimize anxieties by assuring the participants that their results will not be disclosed to anyone outside the workshop.

The number of instruments used should be limited to three or four so that the participants do not feel overwhelmed. The authors suggest that the instruments focus on value systems, personality typology, and/or leadership typology.* Examples of instruments representing these three categories are as follows:

1. "Study of Values," by G.W. Allport, P.E. Vernon, and G. Lindzey, available from any of the following regional sales offices of Houghton Mifflin Company: 666 Miami Circle, N.E., Atlanta, GA 30324; 6626 Oakbrook Boulevard, Dallas, TX 75235; 1900 So. Batavia Avenue, Geneva, IL 60134; Pennington-Hopewell Road, Hopewell, NJ 08525; and 777 California Avenue, Palo Alto, CA 94304.

2. *Personality typology:* "Myers-Briggs Type Indicator," by K.C. Briggs and I.B. Myers, available from Consulting Psychologists Press, Inc., 577 College Avenue, Palo Alto, CA 94306. "FIRO-B," by W. Schutz, also available from Consulting Psychologists Press, Inc., or from University Associates.

3. *Leadership typology:* "Life Orientations® Survey (LIFO®)," by S. Atkins and A. Katcher, available from Atkins-Katcher Associates, Inc., 8383 Wilshire Boulevard, Suite 756, Beverly Hills, CA 90211. "Management Appraisal Survey," by J. Hall,

---

*For commentary regarding other types of instruments that are available, see J.W. Pfeiffer, R. Heslin, and J.E. Jones, *Instrumentation in Human Relations Training* (2nd ed.). San Diego, CA: University Associates, 1976.

available from Teleometrics International, P.O. Drawer 1850, Conroe, TX 77301. "Management Style Diagnosis Test," by W.J. Reddin, available from Organizational Tests, Ltd., Box 324, Fredericton, N.B., Canada.

The practitioner should become thoroughly familiar with the theory base of the instruments selected.

2. *Presentation of Basic Leadership Model*

This step represents the opening of the workshop and should provide a framework and lay a basic foundation for what is to occur. It is the authors' experience and premise that leadership effectiveness is positively correlated with leader self-awareness. In other words, leaders are apt to be effective when they are in touch with their own unique responses to organizational and environmental stimuli and have developed an internalized style for coping with their personal needs and preferences for dealing with things and people at work. Furthermore, despite considerable media promotion of humanistic and democratic approaches to leadership, most successful leaders discover intuitively that no single leadership style is appropriate in all situations; what is appropriate is contingent on a variety of factors that are present either singly or in combination, beginning with the leader's self-insight regarding conditioned responses and preferences and extending to conditions existing in a given leadership situation, including the interaction of the leader, the follower(s), and the setting.

Thus, the authors' practice at this point is to present a basic contingency model of leadership, many of which are detailed in current management literature. This opening presentation should incorporate the concept of *authenticity*: the quality of being in touch with one's individuality, understanding one's true feelings about what is happening in a situation, and being able to choose from a range of options that genuinely reflect behaviors with which one is comfortable. This concept is in contrast to that of attempting to model one's style after an approach that is currently popular.*

3. *Consideration of Value Systems*

Having laid some conceptual groundwork, the practitioner invites the participants to focus their attention on the instruments that they completed concerning their value systems. A combination of discussion and an activity is appropriate at this point to assist the participants in understanding their own leadership profiles. For example, an experiential-learning activity demonstrating the impact of values on behavior during decision making may be employed. However, such an activity should be used only after sufficient time has been devoted to answering the participants' questions about their instrument results. Otherwise, frustration or anxiety generated by these results may inhibit learnings from the activity.

Usually one activity suffices for this step. Care should be taken throughout the workshop to avoid the temptation to overload the design; the participants need time to reflect, to discuss results with others, and to question back-home relevance. If they are denied this time, the effectiveness of the workshop may be undermined.

---

*A good discussion of authenticity is provided by S. Herman and M. Korenich, *Authentic Management: A Gestalt Orientation to Organizations and Their Development*. Reading, MA: Addison-Wesley, 1977.

4. Integration of Values and Leadership

At this point the theories behind the instruments selected to profile the participants' leadership-style preferences and personality needs or characteristics should be explained, with ample time again devoted to understanding. Care should be taken to ensure that the linkage between values and leadership-style preference is perceived as consistent with the model on authentic, contingency-based leadership. In other words, our values generally influence the ways in which we are socialized to respond to organizational stimuli, and these responses—assuming that we are reasonably in touch with ourselves—in turn tend to govern our preferences for dealing with things and people at work in a leadership context. Thus, there is no "one best" style, although through self-awareness and feedback we can and should examine the consequences of various leader behaviors, given the specific follower(s) and situation.

It may be useful to introduce the participants to a model that reflects key organizational variables associated with various styles. For example, the authors have found Likert's four-system model* helpful, although they do not emphasize "System 4" as preferable; instead, they outline the systems as style options that affect such key variables as goal setting, communication, decision making, motivation, interaction/influence, and control.

Again, it is important to avoid data overload. Consequently, the lecturettes should be kept as simple as possible. In addition, careful attention should be paid to the participants' needs and questions, and candor and openness should be encouraged.

5. Experiential Activity

The authors feel that the participants should be allowed to experience both intellectually and behaviorally the interconnection of personal needs, value systems, and leadership-style options. Thus, this step is included so that experience-based learning takes place in addition to cognitive learning. However, if a time limitation or participant feedback indicates that this step should be omitted, the intervention design will not be damaged by the omission as long as the practitioner ensures that the participants understand the interconnection.

6. Discussion of Stress

Stress is often a high-impact factor in the leadership-style equation. Thus, it is recommended that the subject of stress be presented in the form of a discussion of known stressors in the work place, the stress experienced during previous activities, identification of specific stressors that exist in the client system from which the participants come, known ways to combat stress effectively, and so forth.

7. Analysis of the Consequences of Fear

Fear is a major stressor and another high-impact factor associated with leadership style. How people experience each other's behavior and that of their leaders often has much to do with their fears. Therefore, at this point in the workshop it is useful to

---

*See M. Sashkin, "An Overview of Ten Management and Organizational Theorists," in J.E. Jones and J.W. Pfeiffer (Eds.), *The 1981 Annual Handbook for Group Facilitators.* San Diego, CA: University Associates, 1981.

separate the participants into subgroups and to have them complete various sentences having to do with fear in organizations. Examples of these sentences include the following:

- The things that managers do that create fear in subordinates are...
- Some of the consequences of a fear-polluted organization are...
- Some of the reasons that top leaders allow their management subordinates to engage in fear-producing behavior are that...

The purpose of this procedure is to help the participants to express openly the reality of fear as it relates to various styles. During this step the practitioner should ensure that the participants do not adopt dysfunctional or unrealistic ideals because of overreaction to the aspect of fear. For example, it is useful to have the subgroups explore whether their members feel that the fears produced by the "System-1" or autocratic style render it ineffective or illegitimate as a leadership option. The purpose of this exploration is not to promote or endorse this style, but to make the participants aware of its widespread use in spite of the fact that popular literature essentially condemns it.

8. *Presentation of Authentic Management*

This step calls for building on the concept of authenticity in style. It has been the authors' experience that once each participant's self-awareness has increased as a result of the instruments completed, he or she understands the importance of making contact with one's own unique personality, wants, preferences, and tendencies; thus, the importance of not mimicking the style of other leaders becomes meaningful at this point.

In this presentation the practitioner should stress the significance of being certain about one's true feelings and position in a given situation and then clearly conveying this stance to one's subordinates. For example, the practitioner may suggest that if a situation calls for a "System-2" style, then the key to success in that situation is being clear with oneself and one's subordinates about this position. Another critical point is that leaders must develop vehicles for ensuring clarity and minimizing confusion. In the authors' experience, the single greatest management problem is a discrepancy between what a leader states that he or she believes and the behaviors that he or she displays. Thus, it is a good idea to explain that subordinates can more easily follow a genuine autocrat who clearly acknowledges this style tendency than a leader who insists that he or she believes in a participative style but functions as an autocrat.

It is also useful to clarify what "participative" means because this term denotes radically different things to different people. In some organizations, for example, the term is used in ways that seem to convey the notion that all key decisions should be made either by groups or with the approval of those groups, a notion not supported by most advocates of participative management. The objective of this step is to help the participants to focus on genuine, unapologetic, authentic leader behavior as opposed to mimicry.

9. *Reinforcement of Authentic Management*

One or two experiential activities should be conducted at this point to reinforce the lecturette delivered in step 8. Activities that deal with self-awareness, focusing on the present, behavior in meetings, polarization, working through internal conflict, and so forth are particularly helpful.*

10. *Discussion of Back-Home Issues and Opportunities*

Ample time should be allowed for the participants to form subgroups of three or four each and identify specific back-home opportunities, concerns, or problems relevant to leadership style. During this process each subgroup member should explore his or her concerns while the other members act as ad-hoc consultants.

If desired, the practitioner may build into the process an opportunity for giving and receiving feedback concerning the participants' impressions of each other's styles. For example, the participants can be asked to complete a questionnaire on their characteristics as leaders and to share the results in subgroups. If this option is exercised, it is important to let the participants form their own subgroups so that the possibility of discomfort while sharing is lessened.

If time permits, it is helpful to have the subgroups report on the highlights of this experience.

11. *Summary and Conclusion*

This step is a brief effort to summarize the key points of the intervention, to elicit suggestions for ensuring the transfer of learning to back-home situations, and to have the participants generate written feedback evaluating the workshop.

---

*One good source of such activities is S. Herman and M. Korenich, *Authentic Management: A Gestalt Orientation to Organizations and Their Development.* Reading, MA: Addison-Wesley, 1977.

OD SEMINAR
OVERVIEW

Objectives
- To provide managers with information on the objectives and methods of OD
- To assist managers in making decisions regarding the use and potential of OD in their organization
- To increase the potential for initiation of OD for legitimate reasons
- To clarify the types of organizational issues and problems that can be addressed by OD
- To assist managers in becoming more astute "buyers" and "purveyors" of OD methods and resources

Focus

Task
- Organizational analysis
- General organizational climate
- System characteristics (positive and negative)
- Resource utilization
- Norms and values
- Intergroup dynamics
- Critical organizational interfaces
- Management style and philosophy
- Implementation strategies
- Consulting modes, skills, and sources

Interpersonal/Group Processes
- Collaboration
- Conflict management
- Participation
- Openness (in discussing task elements)
- Risk taking (in analyzing current organizational climate)
- Assumption testing
- Competition
- Trust building
- Attitudes, feelings, and perceptions

Target Group
- The entire management system if possible; if not, representatives from all levels of management

Group Size
- Limited to twenty-five to thirty participants to achieve maximum effectiveness

Setting
- Off site so that the participants can be free from work interruptions

Duration
- One evening plus two full days

Methods

- An introductory session is held for the purposes of getting acquainted and generating preliminary definitions of OD.
- The practitioner lectures about the evolution of OD as a field, presents a basic process model, and illustrates this process by detailing the steps involved in specific interventions.
- The practitioner conducts activities and presents case studies that further clarify OD and its principles.
- The role of management in the OD process is discussed by the participants and then by the practitioner.
- The practitioner specifies how an OD effort is begun.
- Back-home needs, applications, and issues are discussed; any remaining questions are answered.

Rationale for Methods

- The seminar process helps to ensure that managers initiate OD in a rational, appropriate manner.
- Managers are provided with a common base of knowledge about OD.
- The seminar content removes OD from the realm of mystery and relates it to solving organizational problems.
- A setting is provided for a candid appraisal of the potential of OD before activities are initiated within the organization.
- Realistic outcomes of OD are discussed.

Probable Content

- One evening for the introductory session
- One day for developing a basic understanding of OD and its process
- One day for clarifying the role of management, specifying how to begin an OD effort, discussing back-home applications, and evaluating the seminar

Practitioner Involvement

- Imperative

Time Relevance

- Usually a first step in a situation in which the organization is new to OD and/or when interventions are likely to affect the entire organization in a relatively short period of time
- Conducted several times in a large organization, starting with top management and proceeding downward through the hierarchy

OD SEMINAR
ACTION SEQUENCE

1

Introductory Session

- Getting acquainted
- Explaining the workshop format
- Generating initial definitions of OD

2

General Overview

- Clarifying the history and background of OD
- Presenting further definitions and a basic process model

3

Intervention Review

- Explaining the basic process model by specifying the steps involved in typical interventions

4

Intervention Activities

- Conducting activities that illustrate the content of steps 2 and 3
- Processing back-home relevance

5

Presentation of Case Studies

- Sharing case studies from the practitioner's own experiences, including an example of large-system change and an example of intergroup team building

6

Clarification of the Role of Management

- Generating data regarding the participants' perceptions of the role of the manager in the OD process
- Adding the practitioner's thoughts on this subject

7

Discussion of Beginning an OD Effort

- Discussing resource requirements, analysis and strategy, pitfalls, initiating options, ways to sustain the effort, and the role of internal and external consulting resources

8

Application to Back-Home Situations

- Dividing the participants into subgroups to discuss back-home application
- Sharing with the total group and presenting any unanswered questions

9

Evaluation

- Assessing the seminar
- Making suggestions for improvement

OD SEMINAR

OPERATING PROCEDURE

This seminar is designed primarily as an initiating intervention to introduce the OD process to key members of the entire management structure, without whose understanding and support a system-wide effort is unlikely to occur. Ideally it should be held off site in a comfortable setting, with the first session held after dinner the first evening and preceded by recreational activity, registration, a cocktail hour, or whatever the organization deems appropriate.

The first full day of the design, therefore, begins with step 2 and the second day with step 6.

1. *Introductory Session*

This evening session is primarily a get-acquainted event. It is best if both dress and presentation are informal. The practitioner should introduce himself or herself and explain the workshop format, emphasizing the importance of participation and involvement. It is also useful to define *cognitive* and *experiential* learning, clarifying that the next day's session will provide a balance of these two types of learning.

Then the participants are involved in generating a preliminary definition of the OD process. This procedure is conducted as follows:

1. The participants are divided into four subgroups.
2. One of the subgroups is asked to list on newsprint the characteristics of the "best" organizations that its members have ever experienced or heard about, and another subgroup is asked to do the same for "worst" organizations.
3. Of the two remaining subgroups, one is asked to list on newsprint the characteristic behaviors of managers in the "best" organizations that its members have ever experienced or heard about, and the other is asked to do the same for "worst" organizations.
4. All lists are posted, and a reporter from each subgroup explains that subgroup's data to the total group.
5. The practitioner emphasizes the highlights of the "worst" organizations as distinguished from those of the "best," indicating that OD is a process that enables organizations to move away from the "worst" category and toward the "best." It is also useful for the practitioner to point out that OD does not define the "best" organization, style, characteristics, and so forth; instead, it utilizes an individual organization's own definition of "best" and assists that organization in analyzing the discrepancies that exist between that definition and the actual situation. Subsequently, appropriate strategies and interventions are chosen to facilitate desired changes.

The introductory session should be no more than one and one-half hours in duration so that the participants do not become fatigued.

2. *General Overview*

A series of lecturettes is presented to clarify the evolution of OD as a field. The practitioner should emphasize in a straightforward manner that OD is a relatively new, expanding technology; that its practitioners are still experimenting with a variety of techniques; that it is not a "quick fix" or a panacea; and that it requires time because change occurs slowly. Because one of the objectives of this step is to "demystify" OD, the authors recommend simplicity and avoidance of highly abstract terminology.

Emphasis is placed on the importance of the process of organizational analysis and the idea that OD is contingent on organizational needs (see Chapter 2). Some type of basic process model that can be applied to most OD interventions should also be presented at this time. A sample sequence of action is as follows:

1. data collection
2. data feedback
3. joint analysis
4. solution generation
5. action planning
6. implementation
7. review and assessment

3. Intervention Review

The practitioner explains how the basic model of OD is implemented by detailing the steps involved in specific interventions. For this process one or two alternatives are selected from each of the following categories:

- *Interventions with a behavioral emphasis (Chapter 5),* including Team Building, Issue Census, and Intergroup Team Building; and
- *Interventions with a structural emphasis (Chapter 6),* including Team Goal Setting, Strategic Planning, and Job Development.

Visual aids may be employed as appropriate.

4. Intervention Activities

At this point the participants are involved in selected activities related to the content of steps 2 and 3. For example, to demonstrate the importance of group participation in planning and implementing, the widely used "Hollow Square: A Communications Experiment" may be employed; to illustrate intergroup competition versus collaboration, one of the many activities dealing with intergroup-conflict resolution may be conducted.*

The activities chosen by the practitioner should be carefully processed by the participants so that back-home relevance can be established and learning transfer can occur. Also, it should be emphasized that the activities themselves are not OD events, but merely vehicles for illustrating some of the critical interface dynamics associated with various interventions. (This emphasis is important so that the participants do not begin to confuse OD with training or traditional staff development per se.)

---

*The activity entitled "Hollow Square: A Communications Experiment," by A. Shedlin and W.H. Schmidt, can be found in J.W. Pfeiffer and J.E. Jones (Eds.), *A Handbook of Structured Experiences for Human Relations Training,* Vol. II (Rev.), San Diego, CA: University Associates, 1974. Other activities that are applicable to this step of the intervention can be found in the same book and in Volumes I and III through VIII of the series.

5. *Presentation of Case Studies*

The practitioner should share actual case studies from his or her past experience with OD projects, illustrating some of the practical applications and preliminary results experienced. It is useful to vary the types of case studies used, presenting one example of large-system change and one example of intergroup team building. This practice avoids the impression that OD centers only on the development of natural work groups.

6. *Clarification of the Role of Management*

Because OD projects generally do not succeed without the support of management and because managers are the participants in this intervention, it is important to deal with the specific role of management in OD efforts. The participants are divided into subgroups, each of which is asked to generate data about what has been learned during the seminar regarding management's role. The practitioner then elicits data from each subgroup and builds on the participants' conclusions by adding his or her thoughts and suggestions about the importance of the individual manager in the process.

It is important at this time to minimize any existing impressions that OD is a process to be led and directed by a third-party trainer or staff person. Without the personal energy and direction of top and middle managers, the momentum necessary to sustain an OD effort is seldom generated. Executives, administrators, and managers need to understand that this is the case. In a sense this point is the essence of the seminar; one of the goals of this event is to make the participants more astute "buyers" and "purveyors" of the OD process. Thus, in effect, the manager is the OD director.

7. *Discussion of Beginning an OD Effort*

In this step the principles and factors outlined in Chapter 4 are conveyed by discussing resource requirements such as time, internal/external facilitation, budgeting, and so forth; the importance of developing an initial analysis and a strategy before proceeding; potential pitfalls; initiating options; suggestions for sustaining an OD effort once it has begun; and issues and options concerning the pairing of internal with external consulting resources.

8. *Application to Back-Home Situations*

By early afternoon of the second and final full day of the seminar, it is important to allow the participants to control the discussion. Depending on the group's composition, the participants generally should be divided into natural subgroups, with participants who belong to the same unit/division/function meeting together to discuss possible back-home needs, applications, and related issues, asking for the practitioner's assistance when appropriate. It should be explained that the subgroups will not be asked to declare a commitment to starting an OD effort. Instead, after the subgroups have completed this process, the practitioner should invite them to share only what they feel comfortable about discussing and to ask any questions that they may have about OD as a result of their discussions.

An optional approach involves altering step 1 by asking the participants to generate a list of ideas regarding what they want to know about OD; posting this list for reference throughout the seminar, dealing with as many items as possible; and then reviewing the list at this point, providing any further information that the participants require.

9. *Evaluation*

The participants should be asked to write some form of evaluation of the seminar, assessing the agenda and providing suggestions for improving future sessions.

MINORITY-AWARENESS TRAINING
OVERVIEW

Objectives
- To examine racism issues as well as opportunities at work to improve the climate for assimilation, upward mobility, and full utilization of all human resources
- To foster equal employment opportunity (EEO) as a way of life in the organization
- To enhance the quality of performance of the target unit

Focus

Task

- Individual and group awareness of the nature and consequences of racism at work
- Understanding of EEO as it relates to individual effectiveness, unit performance, and organizational policy
- Understanding between majority and minority groups at work and development of related goals and objectives that benefit all concerned

Interpersonal Process
- Group norms and culture
- Capabilities for coping
- Problem ownership
- Risk taking
- Openness
- Climate and conflict
- Interpersonal and intergroup trust
- Group/individual stereotyping
- Assumption testing

Target Group
- A natural work group (supervisor and subordinates)
- Minority resource personnel from outside the target work group

Group Size
- All members of the work group plus a minimum of five or six minority resource personnel

Setting
- Off site so that the participants can be free from work interruptions

Duration
- Approximately two days

Methods	• The practitioners and the participants meet to discuss the workshop design and to exchange goals; at this time a prework data-collection assignment is given.
	• An introductory step sets the tone of the workshop and involves a sharing of expectations as well as a reaffirmation of organizational commitment.
	• The organization's present application of EEO policy is discussed.
	• Mixed-race subgroups share the data collected before the workshop.
	• The connection between value-system formation and racial attitudes is presented; then the participants' personal attitudes are surveyed, and the survey responses are shared in mixed-race subgroups.
	• Same-race subgroups discuss opinions regarding ways to advance in the organization and then share these opinions with the total group.
	• Same-race subgroups discuss their perceptions of the behavior of members of other races at work, formulate questions to ask members of other subgroups, and then obtain answers to these questions.
	• The entire group identifies elements in the organizational system that are barriers to interracial cooperation, and action plans are written to eliminate these barriers.
Rationale for Methods	• A setting is provided for supportive and realistic discussion, self-appraisal, and feedback concerning the negative consequences of racism in the organization.
	• A constructive, controlled climate is needed to raise awareness and facilitate discussion of race relations at work.
	• Members of racial majorities and minorities can best explore issues about career-development discrimination, racial stereotyping, and attitudes toward EEO by exchanging perceptions, sharing ideas, and exploring solutions with each other.
	• The climate for and ownership of EEO and full human-resource utilization will eventually be enhanced as interracial groups jointly develop objectives.
Probable Content	• One-half day for the prework session
	• Approximately one and one-half to two days for the workshop, with the second day beginning with mid-course evaluation
Practitioner Involvement	• Imperative that a team consisting of a member of the organization's racial majority and a member of a racial minority be used
Time Relevance	• Either an initiating or a follow-up event for affirmative action/EEO

MINORITY-AWARENESS TRAINING
ACTION SEQUENCE

1

Prework Session

- Meeting with the participants to exchange goals
- Clarifying the workshop design
- Giving a prework assignment to collect data via interviews

2

Introduction

- Welcoming the participants and the resource personnel
- Reaffirming the support for the workshop
- Sharing concerns and expectations

3

EEO-Policy Affirmation

- Discussing the organization's current policy application and affirmative-action activity

4

Exchange of Interview Data

- Forming mixed-race subgroups to share the data collected as a prework assignment

5

Consideration of Values

- Laying a foundation for the connection between value-system formation and racial attitudes

6

Survey of Attitudes

- Surveying the participants' attitudes toward incidents in their lives involving members of different races
- Forming mixed-race subgroups to share answers to survey questions

7

Discussion of Career Advancement

- Forming same-race subgroups to determine opinions regarding the way to get ahead in the organization
- Sharing opinions in the total group

8

Mid-Course Evaluation

- Evaluating workshop progress thus far

9

Data Generation and Exchange

- Forming subgroups to discuss the behavior of the racial majority and minorities at work
- Developing questions to ask other subgroups
- Using a group-on-group configuration to allow minority and majority participants to obtain answers to questions

10

Joint Force-Field Development

- Identifying key issues, barriers, and hindrances in the system

11

Action Planning

- Brainstorming solutions to problems
- Writing action plans that reflect the specifics of the chosen solutions
- Examining the organization's formal affirmative-action plan (optional)
- Planning a review session

12

Final Evaluation

- Concluding the workshop
- Evaluating the entire experience

MINORITY-AWARENESS TRAINING
OPERATING PROCEDURE

This intervention is aimed at a specific target unit (department, section, or management team) and the improvement of its climate for equal employment opportunity (EEO) in its most productive sense: full and nondiscriminatory utilization of all employees as well as simultaneous support of an ongoing commitment to affirmative action, quality of work life, and/or similar goals. The design calls for using employees who are members of racial minorities as "resource personnel" in a workshop that usually lasts at least one and one-half days. These personnel should be volunteers selected from among mature employees who have good work records and overall reputations and who represent units other than the target system. They should be briefed thoroughly about the workshop design and intent before agreeing to participate, and their attendance must be supported by their own unit supervisors.

Both majority and minority practitioners are required, and care should be taken to ensure a balanced presentation with regard to leadership. The practitioners also should be prepared to deal with the deep feelings that will surface during the workshop.

1. *Prework Session*

   During this critical phase, the practitioners and the participants should openly exchange goals, values, concerns, and needs. Members of minorities from within the target system should be excused from this session if it is felt that there are risks involved regarding their future relationships with the group.

   A prework assignment is also given during this step. Each participant is to interview two co-workers regarding their attitudes toward members of other races and the organization's treatment of minority members. The questions to be used should be established and agreed on before the participants are dismissed. Although such questions vary with organizational needs, the following are typical of those that tend to facilitate a useful exchange:

   - How would you feel about having a member of a different race as a fellow worker? a supervisor?
   - Are the same standards generally being applied to all employees in this organization? What are your feelings on this subject?
   - Should our organization give specific consideration to the matter of racial background during recruitment and promotion? Why do you feel as you do?

   In addition, the workshop design should be clarified.

2. *Introduction*

   This step is the first of the actual workshop. The unit supervisor makes appropriate statements welcoming the participants and the resource personnel and reaffirming his or her hopes, expectations, and support for the session. Employing whatever vehicle is deemed appropriate, the practitioners assist the participants in sharing their concerns and expectations in order to establish as tension-free a climate as possible at this early stage.

3. *EEO-Policy Affirmation*

This step consists of a discussion of the organization's current policy application and affirmative-action activity or a brief presentation on this subject given by an appropriate person. Some organizations find it desirable to bring in a high-status person or an informed member of the human-resource department at this time. The primary purpose of this step is to provide some legitimizing background for what is to follow. The exact amount of time spent on this process depends on the level of understanding of the group, the perceived organizational climate, and the previous history of communications. In some organizations a full half-day may be required.

4. *Exchange of Interview Data*

This step should be introduced with an announcement that at this time the workshop will undergo a significant change in level of feeling and awareness. The participants form mixed-race subgroups, ensuring representation from the minority-resource personnel in each, and exchange data collected during the preliminary interviews.

The practitioners should monitor the level of energy generated in the subgroup discussions, neither terminating the process too soon nor allowing it to continue so long that the subgroups stray from the data. It may or may not be useful to encourage the subgroups to share highlights from their discussions; time constraints and the level of participation experienced earlier should be taken into account when deciding whether to invite such sharing.

5. *Consideration of Values*

At this point the practitioners may either show a film or deliver a lecturette that lays a foundation for and stimulates thoughts about the connection between value-system formation and racial attitudes.* In addition, some specific assignment should be developed from the presentation for total-group discussion.

6. *Survey of Attitudes*

This step consists of surveying the participants' attitudes to get them in touch with significant events in their lives and related feelings involving people of different races. Typical questions that are useful in such a survey are as follows:

- When was the first time that you saw and/or became aware of a person of another race? Where were you at the time?
- When did you first become aware of significant differences in traits and characteristics among people of differing races?
- When and where did you last observe an example of prejudice involving racism?
- When was the last time that you confronted a person of your own race about an issue involving actual or potential racism? What were the circumstances?

---

*Information on this subject is provided in a tape by M.E. Massey entitled "What You Are Is Where You Were When," available from Masterco Press, P.O. Box 7382(A), Ann Arbor, MI 48107. Also see S. Simon and A. Carnes, "Teaching Afro-American History with a Focus on Values," *Educational Leadership*, Dec. 1969, pp. 222-225, and H. Kirschenbaum, "Teaching the Black Experience," *Media and Methods*, Oct. 1968, pp. 28-31.

- When was the last time that you openly and honestly confronted a person of another race about some issue involving strong disagreement? What were the circumstances?

While answering each question the participants should be encouraged to recall their feelings at the time and how these feelings affected their own behavior as well as that of the other party(ies) involved.

After the participants have answered the questions selected, they are asked to form mixed-race subgroups and to reveal their answers at whatever level affords comfort. At the end of this discussion period, the total group is reconvened so that the participants can share significant exchanges.

7. *Discussion of Career Advancement*

Use of this step is optional and depends on the time available as well as the participants' comfort levels at this point. The participants are racially segregated and asked to complete the following sentence: "The way to get ahead around here is to . . . ." Responses are collected and divided into the respondent categories of *majority-race males*, *majority-race females*, and *resource personnel*. Then the various responses are shared in the total group.

8. *Mid-Course Evaluation*

The practitioners conduct an evaluation of the workshop progress thus far by eliciting reactions from same-race subgroups regarding what has gone well, what has not gone well, and hopes and concerns for the balance of the training experience.

9. *Data Generation and Exchange*

The participants remain racially segregated and are asked to generate data as follows:

- We perceive the racial majority/minorities at work as having the following tendencies/"hang-ups":
- Questions that we would like to ask members of the racial majority/minorities are as follows:
- We help members of the racial majority/minorities at work in the following ways:
- We hinder members of the racial majority/minorities at work in the following ways:
- Members of the racial majority/minorities help us at work in the following ways:

All data are exchanged while the participants remain segregated. Each subgroup selects the six highest-priority questions of those listed in response to item 2 and then rank orders these six according to importance.

The total group is reassembled. All participants who are members of minorities meet in the center of a group-on-group configuration;* all other participants serve as the audience. The minority participants ask the high-priority questions developed

---

*A group-on-group configuration consists of two groups of participants: One group forms a circle and actively participates in an activity; the other group forms a circle around the first group and observes the first group's activity.

previously, and the two majority representatives answer these questions. Related discussion takes place, with other majority representatives replacing the two in the center as they wish. After all questions have been answered, the process is reversed so that the majority participants plus two representatives from minorities occupy the center circle. The majority participants ask their high-priority questions, and the minority representatives answer these questions, yielding to other minority participants as they wish.

10. *Joint Force-Field Development*

Using the Lewin model,* the total group develops a force-field overview of the driving and restraining forces that have emerged in the data collected thus far, thereby identifying key issues, barriers, and hindrances in the system.

11. *Action Planning*

The total group engages in action planning with regard to the issues and items surfaced in the previous step. The participants brainstorm optional solutions and develop written plans that reflect what will be done, how it will be accomplished, who will be responsible, and when it will be started and completed.

With some groups it is useful to examine the organization's formal affirmative-action plan at this point. With others this process may not be appropriate, or it may become a part of the plans made. The last action item is the planning of a review session to assess progress in six months to a year.

12. *Final Evaluation*

The practitioners provide an appropriate conclusion that incorporates an evaluation of the entire experience.

---

*See K. Lewin, "Quasi-Stationary Social Equilibria and the Problem of Permanent Change," in W.G. Bennis, K.D. Benne, and R. Chin (Eds.), *The Planning of Change.* New York: Holt, Rinehart and Winston, 1969.

GENDER-AWARENESS TRAINING
OVERVIEW

Objectives
- To examine specific issues and opportunities concerning gender awareness in order to enhance the climate for upward mobility and full utilization of all human resources

Focus

Task

- Individual and group awareness of the nature, implications, and negative effects of sexism at work
- Identification of the barriers to colleagueship between the sexes at work as well as the impact of these barriers on organizational effectiveness
- Understanding of the differences between the socialization of men and that of women as well as the impact of these differences on career development
- Development of individual unit plans to improve interactive skills between and utilization of the full potential of women and men at work

Interpersonal Process

- Group norms and culture
- Feedback processes
- Subgroups and coalitions
- Interpersonal and role conflict
- Capabilities for coping
- Problem ownership
- Subgroup identity and individual stereotyping
- Mutuality of goals
- Interpersonal (intergroup) trust, conflict resolution, and cooperation

Target Group
- A diagonal segment of the organization, excluding supervisor-subordinate relationships

Group Size
- Twelve women and twelve men (plus each participant's significant other for one phase of the intervention)

Setting
- Off site so that the participants can be free from work interruptions
- Separate rooms for same-gender subgroups

Duration
- Approximately two and one-half days

Methods

- The participants meet with organizational members to discuss goals and expectations and to plan the workshop.
- The participants collect data from colleagues regarding the roles of men and women at work.
- The participants meet to get acquainted, to review the workshop goals and agenda, and to share the data collected previously.
- Various short lecturettes and presentations are offered in subject areas such as active listening; socialization processes and related stereotyping; passivity, assertiveness, and aggressiveness; career helps and hindrances; awareness stages; and cooperative behavior.
- Between cognitive inputs the participants spend time in a series of same-gender and mixed-gender subgroup discussions, role-play activities, and so forth.
- Individuals and subgroups develop personal and work goals for back-home implementation and schedule a "reunion" if desired.
- The participants' significant others are given an overview of the workshop's purpose, rationale, and benefits; then the entire group participates in a series of related activities.

Rationale for Methods

- A setting is provided for supportive, realistic group and self-appraisal of the negative consequences of sexism in an organization.
- A constructive, controlled climate is established in which to raise awareness and discuss organizational and career benefits to both men and women.
- Women and men can best uncover new and/or subtle career problems concerning sex-role behavior and stereotyping and develop effective personal and organizational resolutions by sharing ideas, relating experiences, and utilizing opposite-gender feedback when appropriate.
- The culture and climate of the organization for equal employment opportunity (EEO) and total human-resource utilization will be improved over time.
- The design minimizes backlash against special attention to women; the concerns of significant others are also minimized.

Probable Content

- One-half day for the preliminary planning session
- Two full days for the workshop (with the second day beginning with an assessment of participant feelings), plus an evening session involving the participants' significant others

Practitioner Involvement

- Team of a man and a woman imperative

Time Relevance

- An initiating or follow-up event associated with affirmative action and/or a program for EEO

GENDER-AWARENESS TRAINING
ACTION SEQUENCE

1

Preliminary Planning Session

- Meeting with organizational members to discuss goals and expectations
- Making arrangements to publicize the training and the prework assignment of interviewing associates about the roles of women and men at work

2

Introduction and Data Exchange

- Orienting the participants
- Delivering a lecturette and conducting a subgroup activity concerned with stereotypical tendencies
- Sharing learnings
- Forming subgroups to discuss prework data

3

Lecturette on Active Listening

- Outlining the principles of active listening and discussing the differences between men's and women's listening habits
- Forming subgroups to practice active listening

4

Lecturettes on Male/Female Stereotypes

- Discussing the socialization of girls
- Discussing the socialization of boys
- Formulating questions to ask members of the opposite gender
- Asking these questions

5

Identification of Passivity, Assertiveness, and Aggressiveness

- Identifying these three types of behaviors
- Role playing all behavior types in a case-study situation

6

Assessment of Participant Feelings

- Forming same-gender subgroups to discuss workshop progress as well as needs and feelings
- Reporting on subgroup discussions in the total group

7

Determination of Career Helps and Hindrances

- Forming mixed-gender subgroups and interviewing members of the opposite sex regarding their careers
- Posting interview data for a total-group discussion

8

Lecturettes on Typical Stages of Awareness

- Discussing a woman's stages of awareness regarding sexism
- Discussing a man's stages of awareness regarding sexism
- Forming subgroups to discuss the content of the lecturettes

9

Key Person's Presentation

- Discussing the implications of sexism at work (presentation delivered by a key organizational employee)

10

Reinforcement of Cooperative Behavior

- Discussing the benefits of cooperation between women and men at work
- Having the participants ask each other questions about cooperative behavior
- Investigating potential goals
- Discussing the possibility of a "class reunion" (optional)

11

Significant-Other Evening

- Having the participants' significant others join the group for dinner
- Providing an overview of the workshop
- Inviting the entire group to participate in various relevant activities
- Planning the "class reunion" (optional)

12

"Class Reunion"

- Reconvening to share interim experiences and to reflect on the workshop

GENDER-AWARENESS TRAINING
OPERATING PROCEDURE

1. *Preliminary Planning Session*

During this session the practitioners and appropriate members of the organization (preferably with both genders represented) discuss goals, objectives, and expectations. The practitioners should stress the importance of excluding supervisor-subordinate relationships when determining the potential participants. Otherwise, a reasonable cross section of the organizational hierarchy should be represented. It is a good idea to explain that female participants should not be expected to share openly their experiences and feelings with management personnel consisting of men who might control their future advancement. Furthermore, no one should be required to attend this workshop; instead, the participants should be those who are interested in exploring the changing roles of women and men, with particular emphasis on relationships at work.

Arrangements to publicize the workshop should be made with these factors in mind as well as the involvement of significant others during the evening of the second day. Invitations should include a prework assignment; each participant is to ask two or three friends or associates at work the following question: "What are your observations regarding the changing roles of men and women at work today?" Responses should be recorded and identified by gender only, and the participants should come prepared to share these data.

2. *Introduction and Data Exchange*

This first step of the two-day session should be designed to acquaint the participants with each other; the practitioners; and the goals, content, and format of the workshop. A straightforward overview of the workshop should be presented, and the authors recommend that the female practitioner take the lead at this point.

One introductory approach that the authors have found successful is to deliver a brief lecturette on the problems associated with first impressions between genders and related stereotypical tendencies. Then the participants are divided into mixed subgroups of four each. Within each subgroup the men and women take turns asking each other to complete such statements as the following:

- I would guess that you drive a . . .
- Your favorite television program is . . .
- Your reading tends toward . . .
- The magazines that you subscribe to are . . .
- The leisure activities that you enjoy are . . .

After allowing the participants sufficient time to exchange impressions and discuss their responses, the practitioners reconvene the total group and invite the participants to share any preliminary learnings from the experience as well as their first impressions of the practitioners.

The subgroups are then reassembled to share the data collected as a prework assignment. Subsequently, common and/or significant responses are elicited from the subgroups and shared with the total group. Experience shows that this process is a good ice breaker in that it does not require an individual to reveal his or her personal values.

A variety of relevant and sometimes stimulating data are often generated in a relatively nonthreatening climate, and this circumstance usually contributes to a positive beginning for the workshop.

3. *Lecturette on Active Listening*

The female practitioner delivers a lecturette in which she outlines the basic principles of active listening and shares generalizations that she deems appropriate regarding frequently observed differences between the listening habits of men and those of women. Qualifiers about generalizations of this type are also mentioned.

Then the participants are again divided into mixed subgroups of four. Each subgroup member is instructed to converse with a member of the opposite sex and to practice, observe, and share feedback about active-listening principles. Experiences are then shared in the total group as time permits.

4. *Lecturette on Male/Female Stereotypes*

The first part of this step consists of lecturettes about the male and female stereotypes that are typical of the socialization of most boys and girls as they grow to adulthood. These lecturettes are delivered by the male and female practitioners, respectively. This phase is most successful when the practitioners adapt pre-existing material to their own personal experiences.* Both practitioners should emphasize that it is not being implied that the participants necessarily fit or agree with these stereotypes; instead, the point is that the stereotypes tend to have high impact on the behavior of many, if not most, men and women as they grow up.

An option is to administer an instrument that provides the participants with some insight into their self-images as related to male/female dimensions.** The instrument results are then used as a vehicle for discussing reactions to the lecturettes.

The next phase of the process is to break the group into same-gender subgroups and to assign the subgroups to different rooms for an hour. At this point the female practitioner joins the female participants, and the male practitioner joins the males. Each practitioner leads a discussion of reactions to the stereotypes presented earlier and then asks the subgroup members to develop questions that they have always wanted to ask members of the opposite gender. The subgroups should be cautioned to ask only those questions that they honestly feel are within the experience of the other subgroup and to avoid rhetorical questions. The two subgroups are then brought together, divided into mixed subgroups of approximately six participants each, and given some suggestions about exchanging and responding to the questions previously developed. This procedure usually generates enthusiastic dialogue, and the practitioners should be careful not to terminate the discussions too soon.

---

*A good source of material on the male stereotype is P. Canavan and J. Haskell, "The Great American Male Stereotype," in C.G. Carney and S.L. McMahon (Eds.), *Exploring Contemporary Male/Female Roles: A Facilitator's Guide*, San Diego, CA: University Associates, 1977. For information on the female stereotype, see R.M. Kanter, *Men and Women of the Corporation*, New York: Basic Books, 1979.

**An example is S.L. Bem, "Bem Sex-Role Inventory (BSRI)," in J.E. Jones and J.W. Pfeiffer (Eds.), *The 1977 Annual Handbook for Group Facilitators*. San Diego, CA: University Associates, 1977.

5. *Identification of Passivity, Assertiveness, and Aggressiveness*

The female practitioner delivers a lecturette in which she identifies passive, assertive, and aggressive behaviors. A hypothetical case-study situation is then presented, with the male and female practitioners role playing each of the three behavior types and then eliciting participant reactions. If time permits, an option is to divide the group into mixed subgroups of approximately six participants each and to have them role play and observe various case studies and then give feedback to each other.*

6. *Assessment of Participant Feelings*

At the beginning of the second day, the participants are separated into same-gender subgroups. The respective practitioners ask their subgroups for feedback concerning the progress of the workshop and whatever needs and feelings they wish to surface and share. This procedure provides an assessment of participant reactions and allows for any necessary mid-course corrections for the balance of the program. In the interest of maintaining an open climate, it is usually advisable that a summary report from each subgroup be shared in the joint session.

7. *Determination of Career Helps and Hindrances*

The participants are assembled into mixed subgroups and instructed to interview members of the opposite sex regarding their careers by asking questions such as the following:

- What has helped you in your career to date?
- What has hindered you?

Data from these interviews are then posted on newsprint and discussed.

8. *Lecturettes on Typical Stages of Awareness*

The female practitioner delivers a lecturette on the stages of awareness that many women pass through with regard to the issues of sexist behavior, discrimination, and related consequences. This lecturette should be based on the practitioner's own experiences and observations and should emphasize how women often react as they pass through each stage. Then the male practitioner delivers a similar lecturette based on a man's stages of awareness. Questions are elicited from the participants, who subsequently form subgroups to discuss the lecturettes.

9. *Key Person's Presentation*

It is often useful at this point to have a key organizational employee deliver a presentation about the implications of sexism at work. However, the practitioners should ensure that this individual is able to be sensitive, to provide relevant information,

---

*The authors have found that showing and discussing a film concerning the consequences of sexism both in society and on the job are sometimes appropriate as a change of pace at this point or during step 11. Examples of such films are "We Are Woman" (featuring Helen Reddy and available from Motivational Media, 8271 Melrose Ave., Suite 204, Los Angeles, CA 90046) and "Men's Lives" (available from New Day Film Library, P.O. Box 315, Franklin Lakes, NJ 07417).

and to avoid succumbing to platitudes. Such a presentation may reinforce the organization's support for the workshop values and objectives and increase post-workshop follow-through with plans and/or behavior-modification goals that are made.

10. *Reinforcement of Cooperative Behavior*

The male practitioner delivers a lecturette in which he covers the personal and organizational benefits of establishing and/or reinforcing cooperation between men and women at work. The participants are then instructed to mingle with as many members of the opposite gender as possible within a stated time frame and to ask them the following questions:

- What might hinder me as your colleague in a work situation?
- What might help me?

The practitioner should state that responses to these questions may be based on impressions made during the workshop if the participants have not known each other previously.

Then mixed subgroups of four participants each are again organized, with combinations of members preferably determined by the participants themselves. All subgroup members are asked to discuss personal and/or professional goals that they as individuals feel they would like to pursue after the workshop. An option is to tell the subgroups that a "class reunion" will be held for the participants during the coming year and that they will have an opportunity to share with their "classmates" any progress or relevant experiences gained during the interim. Another option is to invite anonymous sharing and recording of some of the goals so that potential workshop payoffs for the organization can be determined.

11. *Significant-Other Evening*

The participants' significant others are invited to join the group for dinner, after which a joint session is held for two and one-half hours. The newcomers are given a brief overview of the workshop, which includes a repeat of the lecturettes on typical stages of awareness as illustrations of some of the workshop content.

The entire group is then invited to participate in a series of activities, the first of which is to discuss issues concerning tendencies and/or problems associated with gaining the attention of an opposite-gender group if one is in the minority. Then, if the practitioners wish, an appropriate film may be shown.* Finally, the group is organized into same-gender subgroups, and each member in turn is asked to complete the following sentence: "I am proud of/that . . . ." After discussing the responses, a member of each subgroup is asked to join an opposite-gender group, to repeat his or her sentence completion, and to share similarities and/or differences in the first and second experiences.

If the optional "class reunion" was mentioned to the participants during the previous step, it should be planned at this time. An appropriate conclusion to the workshop is then provided.

---

*Refer to the footnote on page 179.

12. *"Class Reunion"*

If this option is exercised, it is recommended that the "reunion" be held six to twelve months after the original session and that the participants reconvene for lunch or dinner. At this time they should be given the opportunity to share interim experiences and to reflect on the workshop in whatever ways they wish. This procedure not only provides the organization with feedback about the intervention; it also allows for reinforcement of the overall program objectives as well as the relationships that may have formed as a result of the workshop experience. In addition, the organizational climate may be assessed and specific recommendations elicited regarding open, noncoercive ways to improve the quality of working relationships.

PART III

PRACTITIONER CONCERNS

Part III, the final chapter, presents the authors' reflections on several important concerns. The first of these, action planning, is discussed and is related to the crucial question of follow-through. The authors also deal with the issues of focusing on task versus process and client versus practitioner needs. Finally, practitioner effectiveness is analyzed; a number of qualities and characteristics are presented, along with opinions on being nondirective and creative.

FINAL REFLECTIONS

The content of this chapter consists of the authors' reflections about their own personal biases and practice theories. These reflections are presented in the belief that they pertain to at least a few of the issues, feelings, values, and dynamics that are likely to be encountered by any OD practitioner.

ABOUT ACTION PLANNING

One of the common denominators in most of the interventions described in this guide is the action-planning process. In many instances this step is designed to bring concrete closure to a discussion of the data that have been surfaced during the intervention. Furthermore, it is intended to generate commitment to specific action as deemed appropriate by the client group involved.

Some years ago it became disturbingly apparent to the authors that many such attempts at closure reflected less-than-positive reactions and that no small amount of negativism centered in the lack of follow-up with action plans or the perceived poor quality of these plans. Hearing these negative reflections on the substantive results associated with plans developed during OD sessions caused some degree of anxiety and prompted an analysis of their generation.

In retrospect it is not difficult to theorize about these feelings, although there are no easy solutions to the problem. One practice theory in this connection evolves from human tendencies to underestimate the amount of time required to effect change. Another relates to the practitioner's need to be helpful, which frequently leads him or her to insist that every major issue surfaced ultimately result in an action plan. In addition, the practitioner frequently works with highly task-oriented individuals who respond favorably to composing a number of written plans, almost as if the very act of doing so expiates past sin within the organization.

Still another phenomenon that is related to this problem is a certain euphoria generated by working through difficult issues. After practitioners as well as clients have discovered that it is possible to confront these issues, they experience a kind of collective enthusiasm for planning solutions or developing commitments that can cloud judgment with regard to feasibility and practicality. This is particularly true when the process reaches the stage of scheduling events and developing timetables for the accomplishment of specific milestones. In essence, most groups are too ambitious; they want to solve major problems immediately rather than one step at a time over a long period. Understandably, they prefer instant gratification of change needs, and there evolves within the group dynamic tremendous pressure to effect resolutions.

The OD practitioner would be well advised to engage in a candid review of his or her tendencies during action-planning phases, asking questions such as the following:

- Do I think that the group can deal effectively with all these issues during the next several months? If not, why am I not sharing my skepticism?
- Am I too caught up in "the spirit of the moment" and likely to be viewed later as overambitious?
- What does it say about me if I often stifle my concerns about either the scope or the quality of the plans being made? What exactly are my personal practice theories regarding this issue?

Over the years the authors have experimented with a number of approaches to these concerns. Those that have resulted in some success are as follows:

- Suggesting that the group allow a "cooling-off" period between analysis and solution to ensure a degree of temperance that might otherwise be absent;
- Cautioning strongly against overplanning, particularly during a group's first experience with an intervention;
- Reminding the group members that they will inevitably experience a great deal of competition for their time when they return to their jobs;
- Insisting that the group defer assigning a deadline to any plan until all plans have been made;
- Offering personal experience and opinions when it is felt that the plans are of questionable quality and feasibility; and
- Sharing cautions born of experience, without in any way suggesting that substantive closure is not required.

In summary, many OD efforts have been thwarted because of overplanning and setting the expectation that any successful OD event must culminate in a large number of written action plans. Unfortunately, within a very short time such plans are often recognized as far too numerous, vague, or ambitious. Thus, the practitioner would do well to confront these tendencies and to deal with this issue in open, pragmatic ways.

FOLLOW-THROUGH: WHAT KEEPS IT FROM HAPPENING?

Another frequent source of frustration in OD work is the defeatism that is often associated with failure to follow through with even the most reasonable and feasible plans developed by client groups. Some of the causes of this phenomenon lie in the inappropriate motivations for OD outlined in Chapter 3. The euphoria mentioned earlier in connection with planning also seems to have an impact. Groups often become bolder in their efforts after some initial success in confronting difficult issues, only to be faced with the fact that the forces arrayed against them are overwhelming. Group members who previously succumbed to peer pressure to manifest enthusiasm for the plans being laid but who were not personally committed to those plans often reveal their skepticism in ways that weaken the resolve and diffuse the energy of the group. More often than not the momentum dies slowly and quietly rather than dramatically. Subsequently, a kind of subtle guilt syndrome ensues, with members avoiding discussion of their plans so that pointed questions will not be raised.

Certainly another factor that undermines follow-through is related to control of resources. Groups often mistakenly assume that they can obtain cooperation and approval from those who control resources that are required to implement their plans. Still another factor involves the practitioner's doubts, which, if not confronted for what they are, may make him or her a party to plans about which considerable skepticism exists within the group.

Thus, both the practitioner and the client are potential victims of internal and external forces working against follow-through. Such forces may bring about any of several negative results: Poor-quality planning may occur; follow-through may be postponed or minimized in importance; or insufficient attention may be paid to review and assessment of efforts. Any of these results can erode the energy necessary to effect change. No simple solutions to this problem exist. However, it is helpful to be aware of the frequency with which this situation is likely to occur, to be honest with oneself and the client about it, and to emphasize the fact that an initial application of an intervention is seldom anything but a beginning that often must be repeated many times before evidence of significant or permanent change becomes visible. Clients who are involved with short-range concerns about their first OD projects cannot be expected to look ahead. Therefore, it is the practitioner's responsibility to stress the fact that OD efforts require a great deal of maintenance work. It must be clearly understood that no OD project is a one-time inoculation that immunizes the body politic from ever having the same problem again. When this fact is not understood and eventual review of progress produces disappointing results, the related guilt produces understandable avoidance behavior on everyone's part and results in failure.

TASK VERSUS PROCESS: THE INTERPERSONAL-RELATIONS ISSUE

Within the authors' consulting group are several staff members whose primary focus is technosystem interventions, which often require a heavily task-oriented style and focus. Because many groups initially have anxieties about dealing with interpersonal issues, it is easy for these particular staff members to achieve credibility and success by first helping groups to work through task and structural issues surfaced via joint analysis. In contrast, other members of the authors' consulting group approach most client needs from the point of view that until and unless a group has dealt with process issues that are reflective of interpersonal expectations and feelings, its work in task areas suffers.

The notion presented in Chapter 2 that OD must be contingent on organizational needs served to differentiate these two approaches. The issue of task versus process became more a matter of sequence than of substance. However, each member of the consulting group has noted that after working with a client for any length of time in the technosystem area, the focus inevitably moves to sociosystem processes. Although this experience may say more about the authors' personal needs and professional biases than about OD in general, nevertheless it seems legitimate to encourage practitioners to be clear with themselves regarding tendencies to remain entrenched at either end of the task-process continuum for long periods of time. Either focus may suggest that the practitioner should review the degree to which he or she is in touch with the client's needs as opposed to personal needs.

It is easy for the practitioner to begin over time to rationalize consulting tendencies that may or may not be supported by accurate analysis of the client's situation. The practitioner may, in fact, develop patterns of response to data that clearly reflect his or her particular areas of expertise rather than the client's needs. Thus, the practitioner who is comfortable with team building may frequently recommend it as the focus for an OD effort. Similarly, the practitioner who believes that structural change is much more likely to produce lasting change than what he or she has experienced with sociosystem work may frequently recommend job or role development.

One way of summarizing the authors' position is to view the task-process issue as a broad continuum of options that represent degrees of focus on either task or process or both. In other words, no single position or point is always or even usually the correct one; instead, the best approach is contingent on a number of factors related to client readiness, analyzed needs, motivation, and resources. To be unwilling or unable to adopt different approaches is to risk failure at meeting personal as well as client needs.

CLIENT VERSUS PRACTITIONER NEEDS

Another issue that the authors frequently find themselves dealing with is whether or not the practitioner's needs are a valid part of the OD process. In the early years of their experience it seemed totally unprofessional and inconsistent with a definition of OD as a client-centered process to allow themselves to respond to their own felt needs. However, over time it became apparent that practitioners cannot ignore their personal feelings and needs; to do so is to deny their individuality. Therefore, the important concern is to be as clear as possible about what one's personal needs are so that one may confront them either with the client or in terms of the client's needs.

One key to dealing with this matter lies in openly raising the issue of mutual expectations during early contracting and planning sessions as well as actual project events. Specifically this means asking such questions as "What is it that you expect of me during our time together?" Failure to do so often allows the client to proceed on the assumption that the practitioner is the "expert" who will "teach" or direct members of the client system in specific content areas. When this assumption is made, ownership of the effort shifts away from the client and to the practitioner.

The "contract" related to any OD effort has not only *formal* aspects such as specific activities and objectives, but also *psychological* aspects that include various client expectations. For example, the practitioner may be expected to provide evaluations of people in the organization; to tell client managers how to deal with "problem people"; to supply "expert" opinions on handling management problems; to direct various groups along certain paths in solving operating problems; to share specific ideas as possible solutions; to confront system members when certain decisions are being made that involve consequences that have not been examined; or to "sell" certain values, ideas, or programs. Another side of the psychological aspect has to do with whether the client is comfortable with the practitioner's expectations concerning the organization's role. For example, the client may be expected to be willing to analyze and explore tough issues and problems; to take adequate time to determine the real situation as opposed to the ideal situation; to provide a high level of support for data collection and use; to demonstrate at least a minimum level of commitment; and to accept the fact that the practitioner is working for the entire organization, not just the person of highest rank or the contact person.

The authors do not mean to suggest that the practitioner's needs may not clearly involve being directive, creative, and task oriented on occasion. Instead, the point is that OD contracting defines the relationships between client and practitioner and between client and problem and that this process legitimately includes clarifying the expectations and needs of all parties concerned.

ON BEING NONDIRECTIVE

Yet another important OD issue involves the notion that the nature of the OD process, emerging as it does from the applied behavioral sciences, dictates that the practitioner adopt an essentially nondirective style in most, if not all, of his or her relationships with clients. The differences between directive and nondirective styles are clarified in Figures 4 and 5.

Directive (Practitioner as Technical Expert)	Nondirective (Practitioner as Process Facilitator)
1. The client's statement of the problem is either accepted at face value or verified by the practitioner on the basis of his or her technical expertise with regard to the problem.	1. The client's statement of the problem is treated as information; the problem is verified jointly by the client and the practitioner.
2. Little time is spent on developing the practitioner-client relationship. The connection is generally short term and problem oriented.	2. The practitioner-client relationship is viewed as essential to the process, and considerable attention is given to its development.
3. The solution to the problem is generally developed by the practitioner and implemented by the client.	3. The practitioner's responsibility is to help the client to discover and implement appropriate solutions.
4. The practitioner brings technical expertise to bear on the client's problem.	4. The practitioner helps to analyze and facilitate organizational processes.
5. The practitioner is primarily concerned with increasing the client's knowledge and skill with regard to the stated problem.	5. The practitioner is primarily concerned with improving the client's analytical and problem-solving skills.
6. In general, the practitioner accomplishes the job for the client.	6. In general, the practitioner helps the client to accomplish the job.

Figure 4. Contrasts Between Directive and Nondirective Practitioner Styles

Directive Consultation

Position 1	Position 2	Position 3	Position 4	Position 5	Position 6	Position 7	Position 8
Advocate	*Expert*	*Trainer*	*Alternative Identifier*	*Collaborator*	*Process Specialist*	*Fact Finder*	*Reflector*
Persuades Client as to Proper Approach	Gives Expert Advice to Client	Develops Training Experiences to Aid Client	Provides Alternatives to Client	Joins in Problem Solving	Assists Client in Problem-Solving Process	Helps Client to Collect Data	Serves as Catalytic Agent for Client in Solving the Problem

Nondirective Consultation

Figure 5. Consulting Approaches of OD Practitioners

As shown in Figure 4, the directive style of consulting is one in which the client expects the practitioner to serve as a technical resource whose expertise is purchased and who is expected to behave accordingly; in contrast, the nondirective style involves a process consulting model in which the practitioner employs a client-centered approach. Because OD literature is replete with definitions of the process consulting model, it is understandable that most new practitioners see themselves as behaving in ways that are consistent with their understanding of this model.

The authors do not subscribe to the notion that the effective OD practitioner always should behave in accordance with one style or the other; instead, it seems more likely that as the practitioner gains experience, he or she will inevitably begin experimenting with positions all across the range of optional styles illustrated in Figure 5, discovering in the process that certain situations necessitate highly directive behavior. This viewpoint is not intended to challenge the values of process consultation that are widely touted and promulgated in the OD field; rather, it is presented to share the authors' experience that although most practitioners develop primary style tendencies, they eventually find that their effectiveness with a variety of clients is dependent on their flexibility. By experimenting with a variety of approaches, a practitioner actualizes his or her potential as an effective helper in a variety of settings.

ON BEING CREATIVE AND EMERGENT

Although one may hear suggestions at various OD conventions that it is somehow unprofessional not to tailor each and every intervention to the unique needs of the client, most, if not all, successful practitioners develop over time a large repertoire of "tools" that have worked well in certain situations and are used frequently. The authors feel that this practice is entirely legitimate because client needs are, in fact, often alike in important ways. Even allowing for cultural and technological differences among organizations, the similarities among cause-and-effect relationships are striking. Effective joint analysis as described in Chapter 2 does not mean that every situation calls for a new and creative intervention spontaneously developed and never to be employed again. Such a philosophy is inoperable; it places impossible demands on the practitioner to be creating continually and without real necessity. In addition, most would agree that interventions are improved with repeated implementations. This is not to suggest, however, that emergent conditions will not require the development of new combinations of techniques or that the practitioner should "market" a previously successful intervention as universally applicable. Rather, the implication is that the reuse of interventions does not constitute a conflict with ethics, provided that the interventions in question do, in fact, fit *jointly analyzed* client needs.

What the authors do take exception to, as discussed earlier in this guide, is the use of one or two interventions without fail, regardless of the client's expressed or felt needs. It is this kind of poor-quality work that gives rise to confusion about the distinction between staff and organization development as well as to some of the erosive factors that contribute to loss of energy and commitment to follow-through.

THE SELF AS ULTIMATE RESOURCE

In the final analysis, the ultimate tool and resource on which the successful practitioner must rely is the self. Rushing through OD literature and taking voluminous notes at OD conferences may serve only to frustrate the practitioner who does not frequently take stock of his or her personal qualities, values, and skills. All of the techniques and related know-how in the world cannot help the practitioner with whom a client or potential client cannot feel comfortable. Proficient use of process tools cannot compensate for deficiencies in personal skills in such basic areas as active listening and empathy, for example. Similarly, no approach is effective when the practitioner lacks the qualities of personal congruence, good timing, intelligence, and courage. Ultimately, interpersonal dynamics and rapport are more critical to an effective client-practitioner relationship than are the tools with which to remedy felt needs. Achieving personal credibility with clients and potential clients is one of the practitioner's greatest challenges.

THE EFFECTIVE PRACTITIONER

A number of qualities and characteristics seem to be shared by effective practitioners. In the authors' experience, these common characteristics are as follows:

1. *Familiarity with Current Theory and Application.* This does not mean that it is necessary to attend every major conference or to read each new text or article published. What it does imply is that the practitioner does not allow long periods of time to elapse between exposures to evolving technology and thinking; instead, he or she selectively responds to those experiences and ideas that minimize burnout and loss of responsiveness to changing times.

Maintaining this familiarity might include associating periodically with others in the field and attending at least one significant OD event every two years. The authors suggest attendance at comprehensive workshops or conferences such as the "OD Lab," which is given each year in Ojai, California, by the Extension Division of the University of California at Los Angeles; the National Training Laboratories (NTL) Institute's "Program for Specialists in OD," which is usually held in Bethel, Maine; and several events covering OD skills that are sponsored annually by University Associates of San Diego, California.

2. *Psychological Maturity.* This quality is demonstrated in the ability to acknowledge personal feelings and needs. Few effective professionals lose credibility with others by selectively sharing their own struggles with anxiety, fear, remorse, tension, and other feelings. Generally, they demonstrate a great deal of self-awareness and are even more credible as a result. This is particularly true with regard to acknowledging needs for control and achievement.

The importance of seeking experiences that facilitate personal growth, maturation, and awareness cannot be overemphasized. Until the practitioner is experienced at dealing with his or her own defenses, he or she will be less than successful at helping clients to deal with theirs.

3. *Sensitivity in Listening and Observing.* The effective practitioner invariably demonstrates excellent active-listening skills such as those promulgated by Gordon (1980). One of these skills is the ability to detect the *feeling* component in or behind the statements of participants during interventions and other OD activities; another is the ability to reflect these feelings in summary statements that assure participants that they are being heard accurately and supported.

It is also important to experiment with various methods of sharing observations with an individual or a group so that such observations are likely to be experienced as helpful rather than judgmental. The literature in the field is full of specific examples of ways to convey group-process observations. The key to success in sharing such comments lies in timing, tone, and content. Keeping observations brief and to the point and asking participants to do the interpreting rather than yielding to the temptation to draw inferences for them are two practices that increase their awareness and minimize their dependency on the practitioner.

Any practice or training in listening and observing is helpful. Being aware that most people are poor listeners and thus devoting considerable energy to enhancing listening skills can increase effectiveness over time.

4. *Awareness of Personal Impact on Others.* This type of awareness can best be developed and maintained by periodically attending laboratory-training sessions that provide in-depth feedback. It is a good idea to repeat the laboratory experience at least once every two or three years. When on the job, practitioners seldom receive the kind of straightforward feedback on their behavior that they need, even when they request it; clients are either too conditioned to responding to them as authority figures or too afraid of antagonizing them for fear of repercussions. Working almost continually without this personal feedback experience can desensitize the practitioner to the very dynamics that he or she seeks to help others to develop.

Although it is probably not valuable to repeat a basic laboratory experience, it is possible to benefit repeatedly from advanced laboratory opportunities, several of which are scheduled annually by such reputable organizations as University Associates of San Diego, California, and the NTL Institute of Arlington, Virginia.

5. *Technical Background Derived from Training with an Experienced Practitioner.* This background should include co-facilitation in sufficient small- and large-group OD interventions to have met minimum residency requirements. Although no widely accepted criteria exist for an OD residency, pairing with a senior consultant in field work and applying the kind of OD process interventions outlined in Chapters 5 through 7 are indispensable for achieving the background equivalent of a residency. The critique of a responsible colleague in such situations can provide invaluable feedback, without which an aspiring practitioner may never develop credibility.

6. *Knowledge of Both Large- and Small-System Change Strategies and Creativity in Adapting Them to Felt Needs.* Often both internal and external practitioners adhere to rather narrow views and conservative tendencies with regard to developing strategies for change. Frequently these tendencies take the form of focusing primarily, if not exclusively, on one or two units within a complex structure and devoting little or no energy to addressing total-system issues. Sometimes this approach is due to lack of skills, confidence, credibility, or insight. Often, however, the problem centers in the practitioner's inability to raise the stakes with key administrators and executives who are seeking "quick fixes" and simple solutions. To be able to convince such client representatives of the value and necessity of total-system efforts requires an understanding of large-system change applications that combine interventions into long-range strategies.

7. *Ability to Express Oneself Simply and Clearly.* Most practitioners quickly realize that considerable communication problems exist in the majority of the groups with which they work. Thus, the practitioner who models succinct and relevant expression of concerns, issues, and feelings can contribute much to many of these groups.

Controlling the urge to expound on abstractions of little immediate value can be a challenge. Sometimes it is helpful to ask oneself the question "Whose needs will be met by my verbal intervention?" Often the answer reveals that the practitioner would do well to withhold his or her comments. Conversely, providing concise summaries of critical ideas and concerns can be very helpful. There are few substitutes for good communication skills in this field.

8. *Ability to Confront and to Be Confronted.* The prerequisites of this capacity are emotional stability, good timing, and courage. The psychological blocks to honest communication that are present in most organizations often can be handled only by a third party who is willing and able to confront issues so that they are subsequently dealt with. Failure to engage in such confrontation merely perpetuates problems.

The seasoned practitioner eventually realizes the dual responsibility of confrontation and, therefore, invites feedback on his or her own behavior as a consultant and facilitator. Only with this congruence can he or she serve as a model of the level of openness required for effective, ongoing relationships with clients. By demonstrating the courage not to "sell out" in the face of anxiety or disappointment, the practitioner can encourage others to be honest and straightforward.

9. *Ability to Demonstrate Confidence Without Being a Prima Donna.* Clients usually manifest the expectation that a professional consultant knows what he or she is doing regardless of whether they are comfortable with the processes being used. At the same time they are understandably alienated by behavior that negates their concept of a neutral third party who demonstrates objectivity and a primary concern with helping them to help themselves. A practitioner who is perceived to be "on stage" tends to lose credibility over time. Many clients are dealing with a great deal of organizational stress and are not prepared to cope with the added pressure of feeling manipulated by a facilitator who is preoccupied with meeting his or her own needs. To avoid this situation it is important to elicit periodic feedback from clients regarding the status of working relationships.

10. *Willingness to Take Risks.* OD is not a field in which those who are fainthearted are likely to succeed. Many line managers who think of themselves as aggressive and result oriented can quickly sense a reactive mentality and use it to thwart OD efforts. This is not to suggest that practitioners should adopt aggressive behavior. However, the effective practitioner is generally perceived as a professional who understands and is visibly concerned with results, and this image implies a willingness to take the risks required to produce a high probability of success as defined by both the client and the practitioner. Because risks often produce a certain level of anxiety for all concerned, the effective practitioner must be able to cope with the responsibility and live with the decisions that have been made.

CONCLUSION

No OD practitioner has all the answers. On the contrary, most of us are well aware of our fallibility, and, as a result, we become anxious, stressed, and concerned. But usually we can rise above our own concerns and effectively assist others in coping with theirs on both personal and organizational levels, and this ability is what organization development is all about.

REFERENCE

Gordon, T. *Leadership effectiveness training.* Bantam, 1980.

About the Authors

Robert M. Frame, M.B.A., is a vice president of Nielsen and Associates, Inc., of Omaha, Nebraska, a firm of consultants specializing in organizational analysis and organization development. Mr. Frame's background includes over twenty years of experience in both line- and staff-management positions as well as consultation with a wide variety of business, educational, governmental, and health-care organizations both nationally and abroad. In 1975 the American Society for Training and Development (ASTD) named him "OD Practitioner of the Year."

Randy K. Hess, Ph.D., is currently an associate professor of management at the University of Miami. In addition, he is the president of Organization Development Associates and functions as an associate of several consulting firms. He has broad experience in the areas of personnel administration, manpower planning, management development, and performance evaluation and has consulted widely with both private- and public-sector organizations.

Warren R. Nielsen, Ph.D., is the president of Nielsen and Associates, Inc. Prior to founding this firm, he was the manager of personnel and organization development for Ford Motor Company, an internal OD consultant for the University of Illinois, and a member of the faculty of the Business School of the University of Nebraska at Lincoln. Dr. Nielsen is the author of numerous articles on the subject of organizational analysis, assessment, change, and development.

About Pfeiffer & Company

Pfeiffer & Company (formerly University Associates, Inc.) is engaged in publishing, training, and consulting in the field of human resource development (HRD). The organization has earned an international reputation as the leading source of practical publications that are immediately useful to today's facilitators, trainers, consultants, and managers. A distinct advantage of these publications is that they are designed by practicing professionals who are continually experimenting with new techniques. Thus, readers benefit from the fresh but thoughtful approach that underlies Pfeiffer & Company's experientially based materials, resources, books, workbooks, instruments, and tape-assisted learning programs. These materials are designed for the HRD practitioner who wants access to a broad range of training and intervention technologies as well as background in the field.

8517 Production Avenue
San Diego, California 92121
(619) 578-5900 FAX: (619) 578-2042